CAMBRIDGE LIBRARY COLLECTION

Books of enduring scholarly value

History

The books reissued in this series include accounts of historical events and movements by eye-witnesses and contemporaries, as well as landmark studies that assembled significant source materials or developed new historiographical methods. The series includes work in social, political and military history on a wide range of periods and regions, giving modern scholars ready access to influential publications of the past.

A Scheme for the Government of India

Sir George Campbell (1824–92) spent a number of years in the administration of India at a time when rule over the country was being transferred from the East India Company to the British Crown. In this 1853 work, he offers an outline of policy for a future government. He believes that India is capable of being the most civilised country in the world, and favours introduction of the western model of development to India. Campbell laments the lack of co-ordination among various agencies of the government, and finds executive efficiency in an inverse proportion to staff numbers, thus supporting the idea of a small government. He argues for the establishment of an authoritative central power to guide, direct and propel the local administrations. Some of the problems he identified and the remedies he suggested are as relevant to the governance of India today as they were then.

T0345391

Cambridge University Press has long been a pioneer in the reissuing of out-of-print titles from its own backlist, producing digital reprints of books that are still sought after by scholars and students but could not be reprinted economically using traditional technology. The Cambridge Library Collection extends this activity to a wider range of books which are still of importance to researchers and professionals, either for the source material they contain, or as landmarks in the history of their academic discipline.

Drawing from the world-renowned collections in the Cambridge University Library and other partner libraries, and guided by the advice of experts in each subject area, Cambridge University Press is using state-of-the-art scanning machines in its own Printing House to capture the content of each book selected for inclusion. The files are processed to give a consistently clear, crisp image, and the books finished to the high quality standard for which the Press is recognised around the world. The latest print-on-demand technology ensures that the books will remain available indefinitely, and that orders for single or multiple copies can quickly be supplied.

The Cambridge Library Collection brings back to life books of enduring scholarly value (including out-of-copyright works originally issued by other publishers) across a wide range of disciplines in the humanities and social sciences and in science and technology.

A Scheme for the Government of India

GEORGE CAMPBELL

CAMBRIDGE
UNIVERSITY PRESS

CAMBRIDGE UNIVERSITY PRESS

Cambridge, New York, Melbourne, Madrid, Cape Town,
Singapore, São Paolo, Delhi, Mexico City

Published in the United States of America by Cambridge University Press, New York

www.cambridge.org
Information on this title: www.cambridge.org/9781108046329

© in this compilation Cambridge University Press 2012

This edition first published 1853
This digitally printed version 2012

ISBN 978-1-108-04632-9 Paperback

A SCHEME

FOR THE

GOVERNMENT OF INDIA.

BY GEORGE CAMPBELL.

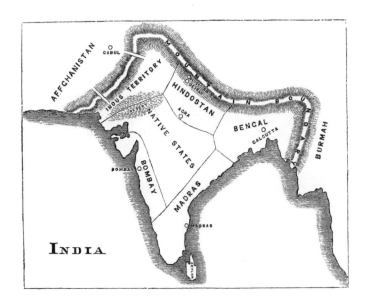

LONDON:

JOHN MURRAY, ALBEMARLE STREET.

1853.

LONDON : PRINTED BY W. CLOWES AND SONS, STAMFORD STREET.

CONTENTS.

CHAPTER I.

HOME GOVERNMENT.

CHAPTER II.

INDIAN GOVERNMENT.

GOVERNMENT OF INDIA.

CHAPTER I.

THE HOME GOVERNMENT.

IT may be presumed that the public now sufficiently understands that the question as to that part of the administration of her Majesty's Indian territories which is conducted at home is in no wise involved in the rights or claims of what once was, and still in name Nature of the question. is, the East India Company. Those rights have long since been determined: the part still played by the proprietors of East India stock in the election of an administrative board is merely intrusted to them for the public advantage; and we are now simply to discuss the form and mode in which India may be best and most conveniently governed, reference being had to English politics and facts as they exist, rather than as they might be under the most perfect theory.

From the peculiar circumstances attending our acquisition of India has arisen a system of govern- Assumed main principle. ment, the main principle of which seems to be so well approved by all parties, as, under present circumstances, better and more practicable than any other, that there can be little doubt of its retention; and it were useless here to argue the matter. That principle consists in the exercise of the right of initiation and the management of details by a permanent board free from direct party influences and mutations, and the possession by her Majesty's Government of an absolute power of control over the proceedings of this administrative body, hitherto called the Court of Directors. Measures of ordinary administration do not necessarily or generally originate with the ministry of the day ; and by the aid of the independent non-political and experienced Court our Indian policy is more uniform, better considered, and less exposed to the vicissitudes of party warfare, than that of other departments of the state. Indeed the more one learns of the mode in which matters are conducted by parliamentary ministers, and of the influences to which they are subjected, the more one is convinced of the excessive good fortune of India, in being comparatively free from such evils. It is agreed, then, that on the one hand some such body as the Court of Directors must be preserved, and on the other, that as, under our constitution, Parliament, and the ministry which commands a majority in Parliament, must of necessity be all-powerful, the cabinet of the day must retain an absolute power of control.

Whether this conjoint government is carried on in the name of the Crown or under the traditionary appellation of the Company— whether the Directors render fealty to the Crown or the Crown exercises authority over the Directors—is of little importance as concerns the Home Government ; but I shall afterwards have occasion to notice the advantages to be derived from the use of the name of the Crown in India.

Name of Crown or Company.

Premising, then, that no radical change can be made with advantage ; that on the whole the Indian administration has not been ill-conducted ; and that comparatively, at least, it is infinitely to be preferred to (for instance) the Colonial Office, we must consider what improvements can be made while we preserve the main principle. I think it will be found that there are considerable imperfections and weaknesses which in no way involve this principle. Although the present machine, complicated as it is, may seem in this country to work tolerably well, it is in India that its defects are felt; it is there that the results of its cumbrousness and slowness are every day practically experienced, acting as a clog and drag on onward progress. We should therefore, even whilst satisfied with the present solution of an English political difficulty, consider the claim of the government and people of India to an improvement of our machinery and acceleration of our pace. In truth, I believe that with all its faults the Home Government deliberates wisely and well, and that the greater part of all that emanates from it is worthy of much commendation. But it is in matters referred home from India for *previous* sanction that the difficulty of obtaining a prompt and decisive answer is found to be an evil of the most serious description, and one which is the subject of much local complaint. Whatever may be the rule in future, it is certain that hitherto it has been considered necessary to refer almost all important measures of internal administration for the previous orders of the Home Government, and that such a reference is apt to be looked upon as a sort of postponement *sine die.* The matter may or may not be revived by answer from England in from one to ten years, but for the present there is an end of it. Many important measures are discussed and changes suggested—all parties seem to approve—but at last comes the too often fatal and conclusive announcement—" the matter has been referred for the orders of the Court of Directors." Now, I by no means impute it to the fault of the Directors that this

Nature of present defects.

reference should frequently be, in fact, an indefinite postponement. That it should be so follows, and must follow, from the nature of the Home Government, from the complicity of the arrangements, the unbusiness-like construction of a large, nearly unpaid, and heterogeneous body, the great division of authority, and the inter-meddling of a separate establishment in Cannon Row. However well inclined each individual may be, it is not to be expected that, regarding a great Indian question which gives scope for much difference of opinion among professional men, and to English minds is infinitely complex, it is not to be expected, I say, that the Chairman and Secretaries at the India House, the Clerks at the Board of Control, the President and Secretaries of the Board, and four-and-twenty easy-going elected Directors* in a constant state of rotation, and without any permanent division of business, or any fixed and professional leaders, that they should all, in any mode-rate time, come to a business-like decision on such a question. There is great security for their doing nothing rashly, but a very great temptation to let things remain as they are; while in fact there is immense scope and necessity for progress. This is the evil which, if we cannot altogether remedy, I believe that we may at least greatly mitigate. As it now stands, it does, beyond all question, very much retard the advance and improve-ment of the Indian administration; and it is on this account that I fear the too great disposition now prevail-ing in this country —" *quieta non movere*"— to suppose that, because nothing goes excessively wrong at home, we may let well alone. I am far from wishing to see too active a Home Government, but I think that we

---

* I give the different authorities in the order in which business comes before them, commencing with the Chairman of the Directors and ending with the Directors collectively.

should render it competent to keep pace with and abet Indian progress, and should secure this much, that it shall not act as a drag and over-check on an efficient Indian Government.

The Supreme Government has at present, according to the letter of the Act of Parliament, full power to act in everything, subject only to the subsequent orders of the Home Government: for instance, it may make any law, but is bound to repeal it if ordered to do so. In practice, however, the communication being now so speedy, and the inconvenience of reversal of accomplished acts so great, it has happened, as I have already stated, that most measures of importance (wars excepted) are referred home for previous sanction; and especially if an expenditure exceeding a very moderate sum is to be incurred, such a reference must be made even in matters of comparative little importance. Now, if it is necessary to wait for the decision of the Home Government, and that decision is not very promptly given, this practice is in fact a deprivation of the power of acting, and it is useless to give the Supreme Government a general authority over the several presidencies if it have not itself sufficient power.

The prodigiously detailed form in which everything is sent home, both by the Supreme and by every local Government, is one great cause of the slowness of the Home Government. Such masses of papers are received that the essential information is almost lost, or can only be gathered by intense labour. This practice, no doubt, originated in the detailed information of commercial matters necessary to a commercial company, but should now be materially altered.

An important question then arises at the outset, of which we must first dispose. Is the General Government of India to be really in India or in England? Are the minor presidencies to be supervised by the Supreme Government or by the Home Government direct; and what is the degree of control which should be exercised by the Home Government over the Supreme Government in India? I think that this subject has not been sufficiently considered. It seems to me that there is not so much question of the relative power of the Board of Control and Court of Directors as of the Home Government generally and the Indian Supreme Government.

Antecedent question — Shall India be governed in India or in England?

It is of the very utmost importance in every way that we should have one efficient central moving power for the whole of India, an active initiative centre, and we must decide whether this power is to be vested in the Governor-General and Council or in the Home Government. We may either intrust the Goverment of India to the former, and leave to the latter only the task of checking, controlling, and supervising its proceedings; or we may vest in the Home Government the imperial power—the direction of the several different presidencies —and merely give to one local government a political power of control in emergency, when time does not admit of a reference home.

When the presidencies in India were detached and separate settlements in different parts of a great continent, they were supposed to have no internal connection with one another; each was governed separately, and the Governor-General of Bengal had merely an exceptional power of control. But when India became one great country, subject to our universal rule, it was apparent that a central government was proper and necessary. It seems to have been the intention of the last Act of Parliament to vest this power in the Supreme Government; but then the Home Government still retained a simultaneous and parallel authority.

While our empire has been consolidated in India, the means of communication with England have been so much expedited that it is now possible to refer things home in a comparatively short time. The subordinate presidencies correspond both with the Government of India and with the Home Government direct at the same time ; and it has happened that, while the Government of India has by law an absolute control over the legislation and finance of the inferior presidencies (the very subjects which might, with least injury, be referred home), it does not, in fact, interfere much in executive matters. The latter are, for the most part, carried on by the local governments in correspondence with the home authorities, whose position, however calculated to digest laws or regulate finance, does not fit them for active executive functions. Now this division of authority is very injurious. What is several people's duty is no one's duty, and there seems to be a great want of executive generalization in the management of India. We must now determine either to make the Government of India thoroughly efficient for the management of *all* India, to relieve it from the clashing of a parallel authority, to subject the local governments to it completely, exclusively, and in everything, and to leave it to manage the empire, rendering an account to the Government at home ; or we must relieve the local governments from a system of double checks and controls which hinder and embarrass them in some things, without prompting them or pushing them forward in others, and place them directly under the Home Government. We have altogether in the whole Indian system too many checks and too little to urge forward and ensure combined and uniform action. Everything is done disjointedly by individual efforts. A Sir Thomas Monro starts up as a great prophet in one age and place, a Mr. Thomason in another; but the results of their experience are nowhere united. They differ in many and important points: opposite systems are followed at the present day, and the right hand of the empire does not even know what the left hand doeth. There is intense centralization of checks, but no centralization whatever of execution beyond the limits of each separate Governor or Lieutenant-Governor. It was clearly the intention of Parliament to remedy this evil, but the object was not sufficiently effected, and another effort to the same end must be made. Meantime steam has raised the question (which has rendered it necessary for me to discuss the matter in this chapter), Shall the central executive be in India or in London? If we lived under an efficient despot, who could at once select, appoint, and maintain a Board of the best working-men in the empire to sit in Leadenhall-Street, there would be, if not a preponderance, at least a very strong array, of arguments in favour of London. We ought to be, and I hope may be, pretty free from wars in future; and for matters of internal administration, the time now consumed in the actual transit of despatches between the presidency Governors and Leadenhall-Street would be (supposing a centralized and untrammelled Home Government, which would answer as promptly and decidedly as the Governor-General) no overwhelming objection. It would seem a good and natural arrangement, that the best of tried Indian talent—now most lamentably thrown away after retirement to England—should be made available; that first-rate Indian ex-officials, whose health has failed in India, or who claim in a cessation of exile the reward of their labours, should be employed in that portion of the government which can now be conducted at home. We should thus obtain a permanence and a concentration of the ability of successive periods, such as we have not had in the constantly changing Governors-General and Councils. Recent practice would from time to time be added to matured experience; the assistance of jurists, too, would be more accessible than in India; and a very efficient Government might be formed. It is true that men might hardly be the same exclusively-devoted and energetic public servants in this country as in India, where, isolated as they are, their whole souls are in their official duties; it is true that in lapse of time personal Indian knowledge and Indian associations might wane; it is true that, while in India a man's physical energies generally decay before his mind, and he retires before he ceases to be efficient, in England a great and good man might decline into senility, and it might be difficult to get rid of him; but still, all things considered, I believe that London might be the seat of government if, as I have said, we lived under a despotic constitution, and could in any way secure the appointment of the best men. This, however, is the difficulty; England is not a despotic country, and it would be difficult to maintain a good despotic government in England. The Court of Directors, as at present constituted, is not at all of the nature of an executive body. Executive efficiency is always in the inverse ratio to numbers; it would be necessary very much to reduce the numbers and to form a permanent Board of paid men of business. Is it possible, under our political constitution, to secure the impartial appointment of such a Board? It is generally supposed that it is not. The number being limited, we must have not only some, but *all*, good men—and not only good men, but the very best men. It may be doubted whether we could depend on so much public virtue; still more may it be doubted whether, if such a Board were formed, they could, in this country, be preserved free from various personal influences. Yet, with all the disad-

vantages, I confess that I should much prefer to intrust
the central administration to a Board at home, constituted
as I am about to propose, rather than to the present
Council of India, located in Calcutta, in a bad climate,
always separated from the Commander-in-Chief, and
generally from the Governor-General, and constituted in
a manner inconsistent with executive efficiency.   But if,
on the other hand, the Council of India be posted permanently and advantageously in a healthy
climate, where the presence of the Governor-
General, the Commander-in-Chief, and the heads of departments may be secured, and if it be rendered strong
and efficient enough in its constitution, then it will be
infinitely preferable to intrust to the Governor-General
and Council the initiative and general executive direction
of all things; and to make the Home Board merely a
deliberative and controlling body, to whom the Indian
Government should be responsible for its acts.

Would prefer India.

Still it is impossible and undesirable altogether to free
the Indian Government from a practical
obligation in some degree previously to
ascertain and consult the wishes of the
Home Government.   The latter must have entire power
over the government in India, and, if efficient, its policy
in large and lasting questions is likely to be more uniform and better considered than that of successive
governors of varied views and experience.   It would be,
therefore, highly inconvenient that, in very important
matters which admit of a reference home, the Indian
government should act without the knowledge of the
Home Government, or without giving it an opportunity
of expressing its views.   I would not attempt to abrogate
the reasonable and discreet use of a wholesome practice.
But I would remedy the evils which have hitherto ac-
crued from it by confining these references to really im-

And what leave with Home Go-vernment.

portant *principles* and large expenditure, by putting them into convenient form, and ceasing to oppress the Home Government with such masses of manuscript and detail, by providing that the Indian Government should sufficiently perform its duty by announcing important measures contemplated by it, and giving reasonable time for an expression of opinion, and that it should not be bound to wait an unreasonable time in the absence of decided and intelligible orders; and more particularly, I would obviate the difficulty by so simplifying and improving the Home Government that it may be expected in reasonable time to arrive at a sound, clear, and conclusive decision on matters so referred to it.

It is with this view that I would consider the details of the Home Government.

First, then, let us look to the form and mode of exercising the controlling power of the Crown.

It appears that at present, although this power is nominally vested in a board composed of Controlling the chief members of the Cabinet, it is power of the Crown, as at present practically exercised by one minister alone. sent exercised. The President of the India Board is a cabinet minister, who, in most instances, has had little previous experience of Indian affairs. He has two parliamentary secretaries, who like himself are unprofessional, coming in and going out with a party; but he has no other responsible and constitutional advisers. His office is at Westminster, at the opposite end of London from that of Board of Control, constitu- the Court of Directors. He seems to be trol, constitu- tion of. under no obligation of personally consulting either his colleagues in the ministry or the Directors. When he happens to be in town he generally sees the Chairmen of the Direction once a week, but beyond this he is not necessarily brought into contact with the Directors; and it rests with the President personally how far he admits them into his confidence. All business between the Court and Board is transacted in writing, which involves the copying, transmission, and re-transmission of every paper. For the transaction of this business there is in the Board of Control an establishment of clerks under head clerks of departments, who have risen, by a long course of service, to that situation. Some very efficient persons are known to have held these latter appointments; but this fact must be principally attributed to good fortune; for I find from a return attached to the report of the Committee of the House of Commons (p. 344) that the subordinate offices of the Board of Control constitute a strictly seniority service, each officer, from the highest to the lowest, ranking and being paid according to length of service. The scale of salary seems to be about 100*l.* per annum for every four years' service. The senior has served forty-eight years, and receives 1200*l.*; the first assistant, thirty-two years, and receives 800*l.*; the juniors, six years, and receive 150*l.* each The experience of all must be exclusively confined to the office in Cannon Row. I am not aware that there is any test of qualification on appointment to this service.

The Board thus constituted has absolute power over the proceedings of the Court of Directors, with certain exceptions; but that power is very differently exercised in the ordinary internal administration, and in matters involving external politics. In the former the Directors have both a constitutional and a practical part; in the latter, three Directors, bound to secrecy, act as little more than mere ministerial officers of the Board.

Powers of; and mode of conducting business.

In ordinary matters the customary mode of transacting business I understand to be this:

Drafts of despatches proposed for transmission to India

are prepared at the India House under the orders of the Chairman and Deputy Chairman, and are sent to the Board for approval, in the form of a previous communication, which is not a mere general note of what is proposed, but a detailed draft, and frequently a very bulky document, accompanied by masses of enclosures. A previous communication goes into the hands of the head clerk of the department, and is by him submitted, with his own suggestions, first to the Secretary, and afterwards to the President. The draft is not only formally approved or negatived, but is varied and altered as the Board sees fit, and is then returned. It appears that nearly one-half of the previous communications (including probably most of the long and important despatches) are more or less altered by the Board of Control; but a large proportion of these alterations are said to be of a verbal and unimportant character.

A proposed despatch now, for the first time, comes under the cognisance of the Committee of the Directors to whose department it belongs; so that if they would make any change they must commence the discussion *de novo*, in opposition to what has been proposed and approved by the Chairs and the Board, and considerable delay and difficulty may probably ensue.

The matter being considered in Committee, the formal despatch is drawn up and submitted to the Directors collectively; but it is not surprising, under the circumstances, that the previous communication, as corrected, is seldom, and only in very particular cases, deviated from. The despatch is now again sent to the Board of Control for official sanction, and this time the proportion of cases in which alterations are made does not exceed five per cent., and in case of alteration the President must give his reasons in full. The Court may remonstrate against alterations, but, having once done so, and received the President's answer, the discussion is closed. The Court may record a protest, but, as a body, have seldom done so.

Everything is supposed to originate with the Court, but the Board may direct the preparation of a despatch on any subject, and when it is prepared may alter it even to the extent of cancelling it, and writing another, which the Court must adopt. The Board has, therefore, *practically* the power of initiating measures, but this power is comparatively seldom exercised.

Considerable delay necessarily occurs in so complicated a system, but the establishments are efficient, and the delays in current business are not greater than might be expected. Ordinary current despatches from India are said to be disposed of in some six or eight months on an average, and in cases of urgency, if all parties agree, the matter may be settled much more quickly ; but there can be no doubt that considerable administrative questions occupy a *very* much longer time, and sometimes in the end no definite decision is arrived at.

Time consumed.

In all questions of peace and war, or of our external relations and connections with native states in which the President of the Board may think secrecy desirable, he has, in fact, the power of setting aside the Directors altogether, and of sending and receiving despatches through the Secret Committee of the Direction, whose functions are, as has been observed, purely ministerial, who have not even the power of remonstrance, and who can only object if the order be actually contrary to law. In like manner, the Indian governors may send despatches to the Secret Committee for the orders of the President. The Secret Committee in no way consists of the members of the Direction most qualified to advise on political subjects, but is in practice a sort

Political and secret power.

of *ex-officio* committee composed of the Chairman, Deputy Chairman, and Senior Director.* It appears that this power of the Board has been very freely exercised. The Affghan war, the occupation of Scinde,† the Burmese war, are all subjects in which the Court of Directors had no opportunity of interfering, and they have even been kept for years without information on matters in the secret department, or have been indebted for it, in common with the rest of the public, to Parliamentary blue books. On these subjects the President of the Board is constitutionally just as absolute as the Colonial Minister or the Commander-in-Chief of the army in their respective departments, and, in practice, a great deal more so, from the much smaller amount of knowledge and interest acting on public opinion in this country in regard to Indian affairs, and from the secrecy of his proceedings.

Appointments to the offices of Governor and Commander-in-Chief are made by the Directors, but must be sanctioned by the Crown, and are practically determined by the Crown, with the consent of the Directors.

The only exceptions of any importance to the ultimate power of the Board of Control are—the recall by the Directors of any servant from the Governor-General downwards—the appointment of Members of Council—the inferior patronage—and perhaps certain disbursements from the home treasury. In these things the Board cannot interfere. They may limit the number of inferior appointments (cadetships, civil appointments, &c.) made by the Court, and enforce the prescribed rules, but can neither name nor veto the persons appointed.

Exceptions to controlling power.

* Young merchants and bankers are sometimes elected to the Direction—young men of Indian experience never : hence the senior Director (in order of election) is hardly ever of the latter class.

† Even *after* the occupation of Scinde the administration was for three years carried on in the secret department. This was a great abuse.

The fact seems to be, that in the ordinary internal administration, the India House, generally exercising the initiative, and possessing a knowledge of details which the Board has not, does in reality form to a great extent the effective Home Government of India, and that serious difference of opinion seldom arises between the Court and Board; but that an unnecessary interference in minute details is practised by the Board, and that the efficiency of the Court is thereby checked and impaired. In political matters, on the other hand, the power of the Board is absolute, undivided, and unchecked. There results from the complication of the system this important circumstance, that it is sometimes very difficult or impossible officially to ascertain the real authors of particular measures, and no one exactly knows on whom to charge the responsibility.

General result.

The extent to which the Indian Minister may consult his colleagues is, of course, one of those cabinet and personal secrets which cannot be made known to the vulgar; but we have the authority of an ex-President for saying that he never consulted even Sir Robert Peel when that great man was at the head of the Government. The same high authority informs us that he would not consult the Chairman or any Director rather than any other individuals in the kingdom on account of their filling those offices. If he wanted advice he would go to the person he thought most competent in or out of office.

Relation of President to his colleagues in the Cabinet.

The exercise of a divided authority is necessarily attended with some disadvantages; but having observed the manner of the power now exercised by her Majesty's Ministers, let us see whether those disadvantages can be any way mitigated.

The present evils seem then to be as follows:—

1. The delay and expense of the double system.

2. An excess of check in the transaction of ordinary business.

3. The want of competent counsel in the transaction of extraordinary or secret business.

Disadvantages of present system.

These evils may be attributed not so much to the nature of the power vested in the Ministry as to the form in which it is exercised. It is evident enough that a double and sometimes treble reference from one place to another, and from one power to another, the voluminous manuscript thereby involved, and the maintenance of a separate establishment in Cannon Row, must cause delay and expense. The expense is not in so great a matter a very pressing consideration; and although the delay is an important drawback, I do not think that the evil thus directly caused is so great as the indirect effect in checking to excess, and acting as a drag on the administrative machine. It has been held that the great advantage of the present system consists in the multitude of checks, by which it is insured that nothing shall be precipitately done. But I believe the fact to be, that in everything except making war (the only subject in which there is no check whatever) we stand much more in need of spurs than checks. Caution and consideration have never been wanting to the Court of Directors, and the only complaint is, that they do not move fast enough. Much of this *vis inertiæ* is owing to the separation of authority. It has been mentioned that the Board in ordinary matters seldom initiates—that duty is, for the most part, left to the Directors—but it is not unnatural, and is, I believe, the fact, that the latter are less willing to undertake important measures involving extensive alteration on account of the uncertainty as to the adoption of their plans by a separate office constantly liable to change,

c

and with which they are not in personal communication. Much of the inconvenience has, no doubt, been obviated by the personal character of the Presidents, and their disposition to avail themselves of the experience of the Directors and to maintain a good understanding; but under the most favourable circumstances, advance is much retarded, and there may again be a President who will pride himself on consulting none of those officially connected with him. It is not the legitimate exercise of their own judgment by the President and secretaries which is to be deprecated so much as an undue interference with details. As I understand it, it is no part of the scheme of conjoint government that the President or secretaries should be professionally acquainted with or informed of details. The object is, that over the proceedings of expert persons reasonable control should be exercised by an English gentleman of superior talents and acquirements bringing merely sound common sense to bear on the subject, and rather controlling what he sees to be amiss than directing what he does not sufficiently understand. He is, therefore, not provided with any constitutional and responsible professional advisers. His establishment is one of clerks, and there is no officer corresponding to the permanent under-secretaries attached to the other departments of the Government. An inexperienced President assisted by a Cabinet of irresponsible clerks can by no means with advantage meddle in details. Such interference must be at the same time inefficient for practical good and offensive to an important body charged with important duties. Yet it would appear that, while there is seldom material difference of opinion between the President and the Court, nearly one-half of the previous communications are more or less altered in details, or what are called *verbal* alterations are made. Now, by whom are these petty and verbal

alterations made, and what are they? A Cabinet
Minister need hardly be employed to correct the gram-
mar of the Court of Directors. That respectable body
can either write English themselves or pay some one
else to write it for them. Still we may assume that
the Minister can generally write better English than the
Directors, and, being qualified to correct their composi-
tion, no great harm would come from verbal alterations
made by him. But is this the real nature of the alterations, or is it the case that the clerks of the Board of
Control are permitted to use their pens upon and alter
the details of the drafts emanating from the India House?
If it is so, I should say that the practice is an exceedingly
bad one, and very unfair to the Directors. The fact is,
that some system of previous communication is probably
under present arrangements necessary, in order to avoid
jarring and official complications; but the result of the
present method must be to give to the Board a power over
details not intended by the law. It is one thing to draw
a pen through a sentence here and write another there in
a previous communication, and another officially to alter
a despatch for reasons assigned. Yet the Court may find
it easier and more expedient to submit to the one in fifty,
than to let it come to the other in ten out of a hundred
cases.*

All this is the disadvantage of over-checking; but the
third evil which I have noticed is the absence of counsel
or check of any kind in the secret department. Wars
are no doubt generally determined by the Governor-
General in India, and in sending orders promptitude is

* Here is a specimen of the kind of interference exercised. The Governor-
General in council lately applied to the Court of Directors for two dozen
of Bramah's patent locks for his offices. The Court proposed to grant the
same. Remark by Clerk of Board of Control:—" I think one dozen and a
half would be quite enough." Order altered to one dozen and a half. Such
is the story as told to me.

very necessary; but still, if these matters are to be controlled at home at all, it seems very undesirable that they should be left so completely in the hands of the President, without the knowledge, assistance, and constitutional advice which is generally available in other departments. If a secret cannot be trusted to a large body, surely the President should at least be bound to consult and have the constant opportunity of consulting some smaller number of selected and qualified advisers, whose opinions should be recorded whether acted on or no. It is certain that in such unfortunate instances as Affghanistan and Scinde the Directors have always held views which in the end turned out to be just.

Such then being the evils, one very simple remedy suggests itself, viz. to amalgamate the two powers in one place and in one body.

If by merely removing the President with all his powers from one building to another some three miles off we save all the delay, expense, inconvenience, and injury of a separate office—if, while we continue and even increase the absolute power of the Ministry, we avoid much of the undue interference with details and impediments to forward progress which result from divided authority, and at the same time insure that the Indian Minister shall act with the assistance and counsel of those best qualified to give him information and advice, we have a great gain very easily acquired.

Proposed remedy.

Why then should not the President be under the same roof and make use of the same office establishment as the Court of Directors? Why should he not exercise his powers in immediate personal communication with the Court, urging rather than checking their progress, fully learning their views, and deriving from them proper and constitutional assistance? It seems at first sight that it would not be difficult to arrange such an amalgamation. Whatever be the relative powers of the President and the Court, it would be a great thing that they should be exercised, as it were, in the same atmosphere. The separate establishment of clerks in Cannon Row to supervise the proceedings of the India House is by no means an advantage, but quite the contrary. Unless the Directors were suspected of abusing their functions (which they are not), why should the President see matters with different eyes from theirs—why should not the same persons who have put in shape their views expound them to the President—and why should he not verbally receive projects of future improvement? Are the Directors such dangerous people that the President cannot be trusted within their influence? Knowledge is to a certain extent power, and so far I believe that the Directors would exercise, and it is very desirable that they should exercise, an influence over the President such as the fixed employes in all public offices exercise over their political superiors.

I confess that I have always looked on this plan as practicable and highly desirable in every way, and that I do not yet understand any insuperable objection to it. The influence of authority *Objection thereto.* in matters of opinion must however be respected, and there is no doubt that some of the best qualified persons seem at present to hold the necessity of continuing the separate office of the Board of Control. It is said that the separation of the offices is required to protect India from the evil influence of party politics. The authority ranged on this side of the question I will not presume to dispute; but I may be permitted here to explain briefly the plan which I would advocate.

All must concur in considering it a most indispensable object to exclude as much as possible the influence of political party and parliamentary pressure, and I have

Explanation and arguments in favour of.

commenced by assuming the retention of an independent Board charged with the initiative of administration, and the principle of a conjoint exercise of power. But I cannot see the advantage of separating by a few miles, and thus detaching the working of, the two parts of the machine of Government. Parliament must always have the power of demanding information regarding, and it may be interfering in, Indian affairs ; and if this power has been little exercised, it is simply because the members have known and cared little about the matter. Of late, however, things have considerably altered : information is constantly called for,* and Indian affairs are sometimes discussed. This disposition must and will go on increasing, as a knowledge of and interest in India becomes more general ; but it will be (I should have thought) by no means greater or more dangerous if the Indian Minister exercises his power in Leadenhall-street, than if he does so in Cannon-row. The only objects are that our Indian policy should not be attacked by one party, because the acts are those of another party ; that power should not be used for party purposes ; and that the Minister should not absorb the initiative management. He should be able to say, "This is not my capricious doing ; I have acted with the advice and consent of the same important body who exercised the same functions under other Ministries." Hitherto there has been indeed this advantage already alluded to, that in ordinary matters, when a despatch is signed by the Directors and sanctioned by the President, it is difficult to fix on any individual the responsibility of its authorship, and a Radical seeking for a victim may

---

* For example I may instance the two enormous volumes published on the Outram affair. The whole essence of the matter, so far as concerns Outram lies in half a dozen pages.

sometimes be at fault. But this would equally or still more be the case if these measures were settled in friendly verbal discussion. If the President officially overrules the fixed and recorded opinion of the Court, he must in either case bear the responsibility, and it is right that he should do so. Besides, it is not often that our Indian revenue or judicial measures are made the subject of stirring harangues in the House of Commons. Those subjects are far too dry, and, if need be, the Government might be well prepared to meet the light. The acts most likely to be called in question are those of the secret department. Till within the last year or two, an idea may have popularly prevailed that the Company had something to do with the Company's political transactions, but that veil is at last finally torn off. We now know positively that the Burmese war, for instance, lies as much between Lord Dalhousie and the President of the India Board, as the Cape war between the Governor of the Cape and the Colonial Minister; and the policy of the Government is as open to attack as in any other department whatever.

The real question consists in this,—whether by the proposed change the actual power and influence of the President will be increased. I believe that not only it would not be so, but that the President would be brought so much more under the salutary influence of the Directors, that some of the present restrictions on his ultimate power of control might in compensation be with safety and advantage removed. I would combine with the proposed arrangement such a remodelling of the Court of Directors, that the President should be no nearer to the initiative than before. I would by no means unite his present functions with those of the chairman of the Court of Directors, but would transfer the initiative and executive duties of the latter to chairmen of committees, and drafts would come before the President only when duly digested by competent persons. They might verbally ascertain his views, and impress on him theirs; but there would be an end to the practice of cutting and carving previous communications.

If then the alteration be made with due precaution to prevent the minister's absorbing too large a share of the initiative and executive business, I cannot see that he will be more answerable to Parliament than at present. I would transfer him to Leadenhall-street, and he should exercise power as minister of the Crown presiding over the Court of Directors, or body substituted in their place. The government would be conducted in the name of the Crown (for Indian reasons to be afterwards mentioned), through the President and Council, or Senate* of the Indies.

There would be no farther necessity for a separate establishment. All despatches received from India and all proposed measures would be in the first instance referred to the committees of the Senate, and by them everything would be initiated, and drafts of despatches and orders would be prepared before being submitted to the President and Senate collectively.

Proposed arrangements.

The signature of the President would be necessary to all proceedings, and he would exercise a general power of veto, by refusing, in his place at the head of the Senate, his sanction to measures approved by the majority; record of the circumstance and of the President's reasons being made. I would make no exception of any kind to this right of veto. It would also be

---

* I shall use the term Senate to distinguish the English from the Indian Council, not as claiming any originality. In this I humbly follow Lord Ellenborough.

necessary (unless the present power of the ministry were to be materially limited) that the President should retain the power of ultimately altering and superseding, on the ministerial responsibility, the drafts proposed by the committees, and approved by the majority of the Senate.

He might, much in the same way as at present, require the committees of the Senate to prepare a despatch or resolution on a particular subject, alter despatches so prepared by them, for reasons recorded by him, and require of the Senate to execute the amended orders. But if the majority of the Senate protest, I would make the Cabinet collectively distinctly responsible, and with this view would require the signature of the First Lord of the Treasury and two Secretaries of State. The method of putting in force absolute power makes a great difference. If the President were permitted simply to present orders for execution in the name of the Crown, he might absorb the initiative, whereas, by the system of suggesting and altering, and in case of irreconcilable difference obtaining the signature of his colleagues, though he may, if necessary, attain his object, he will comparatively seldom exercise that power, and the present checks on the ministerial proceedings will be retained and increased, the more from the President having no longer a separate establishment for the express purpose of assisting him in intermeddling. I would except, as at present, patronage and grants of money from the power of the President to substitute and increase, giving him the veto in these things, as in others.

In regard to the business of the secret department, I would limit it strictly to those things in which secrecy is really necessary, and would have a properly qualified secret committee of the Senate, who must be consulted, and whose opinion must be recorded, leaving it in the power of the President to overrule that opinion on his own responsibility; and if the committee protest, requiring the signature of the three other members of the Cabinet, in the same way as in case of protest by the Senate.

I cannot help thinking that on this system, while the ultimate power of the ministry in great things would not be curtailed, or might even be somewhat extended, the facility of intermeddling in details would be considerably abridged; both the administration would be more speedy, energetic, and systematic, and there would be less opportunity for the interference and influence of party politicians than at present. It is now impossible to say how much the President may have interfered, and he becomes in a measure (when an active person is in office) responsible for everything; whereas, in future, his duties would be well defined, and the chief responsibility would rest with those not obnoxious to party.

Anticipated results.

My argument is that it is not the power of the President, but his separate establishment, that does the mischief, and that, if, instead of living in a separate official atmosphere of his own, he was transferred to that of the India House, he might retain as great real and useful power, and at the same time less habitually exercise a pernicious interference.

I cannot apprehend that the President could in any way encroach upon or absorb the initiative or executive, seeing that the committees who would exercise these powers would be quite independent of him. The only change in this respect would be that the President and Senators would be in personal communication with one another. In such communication it seems to me that well-qualified Senators would be much more likely beneficially to influence the President, than the President to influence the Senators to an undue extent;

and when they agree or differ, it is much better that the members of the committee should know at once how the matter stands, than that they should be under the continual apprehension of disapproval or interference in everything which they may send up.

I have said that I would give the President full power of veto in *all* cases without exception, to be exercised in a deliberate, constitutional, responsible way, for recorded reasons. But I do not mean to include in this clause acts of dismissal, which are rather negative than positive acts. The principle of appointment being joint confidence, a cessation of that joint confidence terminates the appointment, and it is on this principle that either the Directors or the Crown may recall a servant.

This involves the much-disputed question of the present power of the Court of Directors to recall the highest servants, and especially the Governor-General. The danger to be apprehended from allowing the President to veto a vote of the Senate for the recall of a Governor-General is that a refractory Governor-General, and a consenting or collusive President, might set the wishes and legal orders of the Senate altogether at defiance in an irregular way, the Governor disobeying orders, and the Minister refusing to recall him. There would be great danger in taking the matter altogether out of the hands of the Senate. Considerable, however, as are the immediate advantages of the present limit of the power of the ministry in this respect, it is a constitutional anomaly which might possibly cause considerable embarrassment. And I shall not venture to solve that constitutional question. I shall only say, that, if the anomaly can be got over, it is very desirable that both the Senate and the Crown should separately have the power of dismissing any servant either in India or in England. In any case the rule must be reciprocal, either that each may dismiss or that both must concur in dismissing. I think, however, that it would be well to require a concurrence of three-fourths of the Senate in a vote for the dismissal of a Governor-General, if they are permitted to exercise that power independent of the Crown.

I should say that a control or veto over all inferior appointments made by the Senate might be exercised by the Minister without danger and with considerable benefit, and that it should be his special charge to see that no unfit persons are sent out.

If, however, it be decided that it is impossible to *If remedy rejected, minor improvements suggested.* unite under one roof the Board of Control and Court of Directors, that the President must still be kept apart, and must still have a separate office establishment, it might be well to do something either to limit the practice of interfering in details, or to provide responsible advisers of the President in such interference.

Some previous communication of intended measures may, no doubt, be advantageous, but it should be confined to a general note of the proposed arrangements to pass between the heads of the India House Committees and the President and Secretaries of the Board, whose *English* intellects are to be brought to bear on it. The *detailed* previous communication of a despatch, to be subjected to the *professional* criticism of the Board of Control establishment, might, I should think, with advantage be discontinued; and when a despatch is officially sent up for sanction, the Board's duties should be confined to approval, disapproval, or material alteration, for written reasons assigned. There should be no interference, without specified reasons, in smaller matters, or in anything in which the President and Parliamentary Secretaries do not think themselves, *unaided*, competent to overrule the judgment of the Senators. The chairmen of committees should have every facility of personally communicating with the President.

Or if it be considered right that every despatch should be *professionally* revised and criticised by a separate establishment, there should be added to the Board either additional paid and professional members, or permanent competent and responsible under-secretaries, who might stand forth to the world as exercising a large share of the government of India, instead of being shrouded in the mysteries of a bureaucracy.

In the secret department, an efficient secret committee being provided at the India House, their opinions should be given and recorded as formerly proposed, the President having the option, in case of emergency, of transmitting orders after hearing their arguments for the space of one hour and considering for one day, of which proceeding minutes should be made.

Next we are to consider the constitution of that administrative Court, or Council, or Senate, which all agree must continue to form an essential part of the system. A great part of the present functions of the Court of Directors (especially in regard to the inferior presidencies) being transferred to the Indian Government, and business being only reported or referred home in a more advanced stage, great part of the objection to the present Court would cease to be tenable, and it would undoubtedly be a good deliberative body, containing within itself a great mass of Indian knowledge and experience. But the question is, can it not be made better? Its constitution is in many respects faulty.

It may be no great evil that there are many members of the Court whose absence would not be felt. If they do no good, they also do little harm.

But a very great and crying evil, and one which most assuredly demands a remedy, is that fact which is admitted on all hands, viz. that, while a numerous Board for the management of Indian affairs exists, the majority of the most efficient public servants who come from India in the prime of life and intellect are by the present system absolutely excluded from

Evil of exclusion of most fit men. any share in Indian affairs. It is quite lamentable to see the men who, after surviving five-and-twenty years of incessant labour in exile in a tropical climate, think themselves entitled to retire to their native country before it is too late—the very best men of a great profession, trained to business from their youth upwards—men who have ruled kingdoms and determined the destinies of millions of their fellow-creatures — to see them at five-and-forty sinking down into small country gentlemen with nothing to do, or into careless water-drinking old Indians. One feels that there must be something wrong when one reads *obscure* among obscure Buckinghamshire magistrates such a name as that of Robert Mertins Bird, familiar as their household gods to some five-and-twenty millions of Asiatics whose all-important interests have been regulated by him, but whose existence is almost unknown in this country. There is no lack of work for men of business in the service of England. The civil service of the state in its higher departments was never a regular profession, and since the Reform Bill has ceased to be professed at all. We depend for everything on accidental or amateur talent. But Indians (who alone of Englishmen have followed this profession) do not make fortunes now-a-days. Parliament is seldom open to them : the avenues of occupation and advancement are therefore closed, and they live but on the past. Surely the Indian home administration should from so great a supply be well filled. Here, at least, should be a useful occupation for the great men of the East. Unfortunately the Direction can only be entered by election. Election can only be attained by canvassing for years the most sweet voices of the proprietors of East India stock; by continued harassing labour, personal humiliation, and city connection. The best men generally think that they have purchased exemption from the first of these requisites; they have little taste for the second; they are seldom possessed of the third; and I may add, that the position of a Director, partly owing to the vexatious power exercised by the clerks of the Board of Control, and partly to the constitution of the Court itself, is not such as to make it, except as a source of patronage, the great object of ambition which it ought to be to the most distinguished of retiring Indians. It is therefore a fact beyond dispute, that in most cases they prefer to subside into insignificance.

A canvass for the East India Direction generally lasts about seven years. It is sometimes asserted that eminent men have got in, and may get in, with comparatively little trouble; but that statement is not borne out by facts. There are a few instances of very distinguished men who have come in, not with little trouble, but with less than the average labour. One in particular is adduced of a man very eminent in the Indian service, who was elected before he had been three years at home; but I believe that in every such instance the eminence will be found to have been combined with the accident of connection and interest, and that these cases are the exception, not the rule. As the instance to which I have most particularly referred has been quoted to the Committees of Parliament, and is the strongest—indeed, I may say, the only one—on that side of the question, I would venture to recommend that that eminent man should himself be sent for, and asked—first, whether, even in his case, the canvass was a light matter; and, second, whether in his opinion he would, with all his eminence, have come in nearly so soon if he had not been powerfully backed by a strong personal connection and interest among the voters. No one has a more lively sense of the disagreeables of the approach to the Direction than those who have surmounted them and got in; and I believe the fact to be, that the difficulties are increasing every day; that the evil is a rapidly growing one. Indeed, the canvassing system is now carried so far, that the electors have it not in their power to elect the best man when a vacancy occurs. They are pledged five or six deep; and when a new candidate comes from India they may be obliged to say, "I admit your claims; I would vote for you if I could, but I am already pledged to so many that I cannot do so for a number of years to come."

In practice, it is the fact that the majority of the Directors are now men who have had more or less experience in India, and that there are among them some highly distinguished and many very good and much to be respected men, but still they are not elected, by any means, according to the measure of fitness; nor can any man get in except by a most protracted and unpleasant struggle (to which the patronage is the principal inducement), and till the very years in which, fresh from the scene, he might be most useful have passed away. There are also a considerable number of Directors who have no Indian experience whatever. Their holding the office is justified on the ground of the advantage of having an admixture of the leaven of English minds in the Court. And the argument is doubtless a very sound one, if we suppose working English men of business to be introduced as active members of the Court. But what is the fact? I believe that the English Directors are, without exception, merchants and bankers of the city—men who have affairs of their own to attend to, which are to them infinitely more important, who take office for the sake of the patronage, and through city influence. They were, no doubt, the most fitting directors of a commercial company; but I confess that for the government of India I can see no advantage in their filling many places at the Board while so many experienced men are excluded. It is every way desirable to have in the Direction one or two Englishmen from each of several classes, but not a large number of one particular class.

Much of what is wanting to the efficiency of the Court of Directors, and to the position of a Director, is owing to the internal constitution of the Court; and the defects principally arise from arrangements which were very proper for the management of the affairs of a great joint-stock company, but which have become quite inappropriate to the government of an empire. The Directors are nominally elected for four years, but virtually (by a system of combination) for life. Each must remain out one year in five; so that there are really thirty Directors, of whom six are always out by rotation, and all are continually changing their relative positions (as if they were annually shaken up together in a hat *Evils resulting from commercial constitution of East India Direction.* or a kaleidoscope) in a way which must go far to destroy their efficiency. The body is too numerous to do business, in the first instance, collectively. It is divided into committees, who take up different subjects; but these committees are every year appointed by rotation, so that a financier is one year on the judicial, and the next on the military committee, and no one has any chance of a continued supervision of a particular department. Even the committees, such as they are, are only, as it were, consultative committees. The whole initiative and executive seem to be nominally in the hands of the Chairman and Deputy-Chairman, and practically for the most part (except when there happens to be a remarkably efficient Chairman) in those of the subordinate establishment. The Chairs are elected each year by the Directors, and are almost invariably changed each year. I think I may say that they are elected rather with reference to their personal qualifications to preside over a miscellaneous body of Englishmen, and to make a good figure in transactions at home, than as signifying an opinion that they are the Directors most qualified to govern India, and also that most Directors have some time or other their turn of filling the Chair, whether they have Indian experience or not. I understand that the Director who will occupy that post in the ensuing last year of the present term has never been in India, and that the business of the East India Direction is not his profession or his most important avocation.

For the transaction of business there is at the India House a large and efficient establishment of secretaries, examiners, and clerks. This home service of the Company does not seem to follow any strict rule of seniority; but I do not know that there is more than one instance of a retired Indian servant now employed. It generally consists of Englishmen of business employed by the Court of Directors, most of whom make it the profession of their lives; while others are specially entertained. To all despatches received from India answers are prepared by the departmental officers of the India House establishment, under the direction of and in communication with the Chair and Deputy Chair; and this is the previous

East India House establishment.

communication which, as I have before noticed, is sent to the Board of Control, there corrected, and generally settled between the Board and the Chairs, before the Committee see it at all. If the Chair and Deputy Chair do not happen to be Indian professional men, acquainted with the particular subject under discussion, it must be of necessity that the management of details is much more in the hands of the subordinate officers than in those of the Committee, to whom a matter goes after all other parties have expressed their opinion, and with whom therefore, in fact, rests only a power of remonstrance, very useful, no doubt, when the object was to see that their money was not misspent, but hardly sufficient for the duty of managing a great department.

For that part of the system which excludes from the Direction all Indian officers, whatever their qualifications, who do not care to canvass for years, and do not canvass with success, some remedy is absolutely necessary. *Remedies for exclusion of best men from Direction.* What shall it be? You must first, by diminishing the patronage and raising the official position of a Director, make a seat in the Direction less an object to ordinary influence—less a valuable subject of canvass, and more an object of honest ambition to official men. Then as to the mode of appointment. The only two methods of constituting Directors are election and nomination. First, then, can the mode of election be altered for the better? and secondly, can any plan of nomination be substituted? I must say that I much doubt the possibility of very greatly improving the mode of election, for this reason: that all kinds of schemes have been propounded, and there is not one which meets any degree of general favour as an improvement, while in most there would be a decided deterioration. All these schemes propose alterations either in the qualification of voters, or the mode of voting.

It has been proposed to give votes to retired servants of the Company, and also to holders of stock in the Proposed
changes in
qualification
of voters. Indian funds. But to both of these plans there is this insuperable objection—that it would inevitably lead to men laying themselves out for the Direction, if not openly canvassing for votes while still in India. The army forms the great numerical majority of the Indian service, and, under Lord Ellenborough's proposed plan, the Directors would be simply the men most popular with the army. Not only is there a constant stream of retirements, but those out of the service are so intimately connected with those still in it, that the opinion and influence of the army in India would be all powerful with the retired body at home. Popularity is not always the best test of efficiency ; and can anything be conceived more prejudicial to discipline and injurious in every way than a general officer, holding high office in an army, striving to secure his return to the Direction a few years subsequently, like the American Commander-in-Chief canvassing and inspecting at the same time? Again, take the other plan. The holders of Indian stock are principally in India, and a large proportion are natives. Conceive a member of Council, or the head of a department in a Government constituted like that of India, devoting his time to canvassing the voices of the Baboos in order to secure his election on his retirement! Nothing could be more pernicious. This objection, however, does not apply to holders of Indian funds resident in England.

Another proposition is to give votes to English fund-holders. There would be no objection on principle to that plan, but it would only make the canvass a more serious affair than ever.

In short, seeing that whichever way we turn to look for an improved constituency we only make matters worse—or, at any rate, no better; that the proprietors of East India stock are just as good a constituency as we are anywhere likely to find; that they have in their favour the prescription of having long exercised this power; and that the desire to possess a vote has doubtless attracted to this description of stock many persons interested in India, I think that we had better be content with the voters that we have, than fly to others that we know not of. But I should see no insuperable obstacle to adding to the constituency the holders of a certain sum (say 20,000 rupees) in the Indian funds resident in England, and such an arrangement would go far to mitigate the exclusive power now possessed by the *City* interest.

It may still be a question whether the mode of voting can be improved. It seems that proxies are only permitted if executed a certain number of days before the poll; and it is proposed to extend the time, that natives of India may become voters. To this the same objection applies which I have urged to the plan of the Indian fundholders being intrusted with votes. There would be no harm in natives having votes, but there would be the greatest possible harm in officers of Government soliciting their votes.

Proposed changes in mode of voting.

A Director has propounded a scheme of electoral colleges, and, when I first heard of it, I fancied that it was one for dividing the electors into separate constituencies, instead of electing the Directors collectively; but on looking at the plan, as explained to the committee, it turns out to be something quite different, and so far beyond my poor comprehension that I cannot venture to hint a decided opinion concerning it. I confess that the difficulty of making apparent to ordinary understandings how the best men are to be thereby secured seems to me a *primâ facie* objection ; and as to its operation in the Royal Society, it must be remembered that that body has no cadetships to dispose of, and that the same practical value does not attach to its offices as to an East India directorship. Though I am not sure that it has been authoritatively put forth, I cannot help thinking that the division into constituencies might be the only practicable improvement ; so that the present system of *combination* might be in some degree interfered with, and the canvass might be more limited and less protracted. I am supposing each constituency of proprietors to elect a Senator for life, or for a very long term of years, and, on a vacancy, that constituency to elect another, so that it might be more like canvassing a small borough. If the tenure be for life, the plan might answer, and, when a Senator unexpectedly dies, the candidates would have a short vigorous fight, and have done with it. But if re-elections take place at stated periods, I confess that I think the value of the patronage would make it altogether unlike a parliamentary election, and that there must be one unceasing canvass and barter of patronage for votes.

Take it as we may, the fact is simply this—that by no form of election can you possibly secure the best men. You may get a large proportion of good men, but can never depend on always having the best. Electors will never, when electing a distributor of patronage, choose *solely* on public grounds (why should they ?) ; and there are many men eminently fitted for the business of government, but eminently unfitted for a popular candidature.

Insufficiency of all these proposals.

The alternative is nomination, and I must say that I do not see the force of the insuperable objection which many people entertain to intrusting a very limited power of this kind to the Government of the day. I do not see why, as vacancies occur, the Government should not present to a certain proportion of the seats from among persons of a certain service and prescribed Indian qualification : that is, in fact, from a limited profession, in the same way as her Majesty's judges are appointed, and on the same tenure ; and with the concurrence of the existing Senate.

Proposed nomination of a portion of the Senators.

May it.not be that, in a feeling of reaction from the abuses of the past, we run to the other extreme of too much distrusting the Government ? Do we not, in some degree, confound abuse of patronage in the creation of unnecessary offices and emoluments, or the omission of necessary duties for the sake of patronage, with its use in filling, under proper restrictions, in the light of day, and subject to the judgment of popular opinion, legitimate and necessary offices ? Though most anxious to see a radical reform of abuses, I am conservative enough to wish for a strong Government ; and it strikes me that Governments of the present day, far from having too much power, have too little ; that they have, as it were, too little ballast ; that the *ins*, as a matter of course, become gradually unpopular, and the wheel revolves more and more speedily. In this view, the exercise of *legitimate* patronage by the Government is anything but a disadvantage, and is the best safeguard against the creation and abuse of illegitimate patronage. You cannot altogether muzzle the oxen that tread out the corn. The only question is, how far the proposed arrangement is liable to abuse? Now, we must admit that *non-professional* appointments—those to which any one may be appointed—are still, even if not grossly abused,

most frequently given away rather by personal favour
than by merit; but wherever the choice is limited, and
the candidates are known, in all professional appointments, I believe that public opinion is now an amply
sufficient safeguard, and that gross abuse is rarely met
with. Take all the higher legal, and I will even go so
far as to say clerical appointments. Of two qualified
candidates for a judgeship, one on the right side may,
no doubt, be generally preferred (and even this consideration is, I imagine, in some instances little attended
to), but the appointment is never made matter of mere
patronage and never abused. Is there any recent case
in which any Ministry have ever been even accused of
wilfully making a bad judge? Have not even the
bishops been generally respectable men, till they attained
that elevation so dangerous to all human virtue? And
great as is the patronage held by bishops, it is by no
means indirectly exercised by the Ministry; bishops use
their patronage for personal, but not for political objects.
Might not Senators be nominated the same way as
judges are nominated? From a limited profession, from
persons who have served a certain time in that profession, and who can produce testimony of their efficiency, I
would nominate a certain number of professional working
Senators, and the appointments should be for life—or
for so long as the incumbents are fit for the duties—and
with a retiring pension. I would give two-thirds of the
Senate a power of veto, or rather would require the concurrence of one-third in the election of a person named
by the Crown in a *congé d'élire*. It would follow that
no one Ministry would have the appointment of all or
of many Senators. When a vacancy occurred, the
party in office would nominate; they might consider
politics as much as they do in a judgeship; but even
this is not probable, as Indians so seldom take part in

politics. I hardly think that it would be a disadvantage if there was some additional stimulus to induce retired Indians to get into Parliament, and take a part there. If a very unfit person were nominated, he would be excluded by the Senate. I do, then, believe that such a mode of nomination would not be seriously abused in the present day, and that the services would be made available of many distinguished and efficient men, who are now excluded from the Direction. It must be remembered, in addition to other arguments, that, as I would very much reduce the value of a Senator's patronage, and would not make the salary high, there would be much less temptation to job the appointment away. It is urged that public opinion would not tell with the same force on Indian professional appointments as on appointments from professions in this country—and no doubt the press and the public would not be *so* all-powerful; but still there is now a very strong Anglo-Indian public, and it would be amply represented in the press. I believe, therefore, that it would be sufficiently powerful to prevent any very great abuse in so public and important a matter as the appointment of a Senator. I do not suppose that you would get *only* the best men, but I think that, if the position of a Senator were at the same time made what it ought to be, you would have all the *most* distinguished men, and no *very unfit* ones. Under such a system, Elphinstone, Mackenzie, and R. M. Bird, would have been long ago members of the Direction, and, between election and nomination, you would have secured a sufficient proportion of the most fit'men.

Whatever be thought of details, some system of joint nomination by concurrence of the Crown and the existing Senate is certainly necessary.

Still it is, no doubt, desirable to limit as much as possible the risk of abuse. A limit of selection to those whose service in India has been efficient would be most useful. Lord Ellenborough's plan, by which Senators are to be nominated in the first instance by the Governor-General in India, is not explained in detail; and I do not see that practically it can come to anything beyond this: that the Governor-General should have it in his power to place publicly on record, when a public servant leaves India, his opinion of that servant's fitness for further service at home; leaving that recommendation to weigh with the Ministry and on public opinion *quantum valeat*. Something of this kind would, no doubt, be very useful. It would not do to permit a single Governor-General to exclude a man for ever from the Senate; but I would make a certificate of fitness indispensable to nominees—would give the power of granting such certificates in favour of persons who have filled certain offices both to the Governor-General in India and to the Senate at home—and would thus form a class of " emeriti," from whom the Government should be bound to select.

Another plan is, that the Senate should select, and the veto should rest with the Crown; but to this I object, that, as the existing Directors have already a very great influence in the elections, the Senate would be on this system too much of a close corporation.

If objection be made to nominating Senators for life, because they might get old without retiring, I answer, first, that the present Directors do in fact hold for life, so that nothing is lost in this respect; second, that you don't want *too* much personal activity in the Home Government, the active Government being in India; third, that it is the only possible way of securing the independence of the Senators; and fourth, that by providing a retiring pension you may superannuate Senators as you do Judges, and that I would superannuate them after a certain age.

If the Senators were *all* nominated, a smaller number would suffice: but as it is probable that some elected members will be retained (and it is desirable that it should be so),—as all of these latter will not be working members, and the collective body will be more deliberative than executive,—I think that the present number of twenty-four might, without detriment, be retained. It must not, however, be forgotten that, as the six *out* Directors have, *de facto*, just as much interest in the Direction as the twenty-four who are now in, there are at present thirty members of the Court to be disposed of; but in that number there must be some whose age, health, or avocations prevent them from taking a very active part; and it might either be arranged to name the twenty-four to remain in, in the Act of Parliament, excluding the six who have hitherto taken least part; or a general election might take place, to give the proprietors the opportunity of selecting those among the thirty whom they would choose to retain; or the six might be retained for a time as supernumeraries.

If possible, still more necessary than a change in the mode of appointing Directors, is a reform and remodelling of the internal constitution, &c., of the Direction.

The nature of the improvements in the interior arrangements and mode of conducting business, embodied in the changes which I am about to suggest, will be evident without farther explanation. And I may here say, that all the proposed improvements in the Court of Directors will be equally applicable even if it is determined to maintain the separate office in Cannon Row, and will still very largely influence the efficiency of the Indian Government.

I would propose then as follows:—

1. The title of the Court of Directors to be changed to that of "Senate of the Indies," the present twenty-four Directors to be the first senators.

Summary of proposed Home Government.

2. The commercial constitution and rules of the Court to be at the same time altogether altered.

3. A minister of Indian affairs, holding office at the pleasure of the Crown, to be ex-officio President of the Senate, and chairman of the political committee.

4. To the eight next vacancies, other than vacancies by rotation, nominations shall be made as they occur by the Crown, in a *congé d'élire*, from among persons who have served the Government in India for not less than ten years, who have filled certain superior offices (to be afterwards particularised) for not less than two years—who have been absent from India, or retired from the service, not more than ten years—whose age does not exceed sixty years—and who on retirement have been declared to be emeriti either by the Senate or by the Indian Supreme Government. The present Senate and ex-Governors-General to have the power of granting such certificates to persons already retired. The certificates to state that the recipient has done remarkably good service to the state in a superior office, and is well fitted for farther important service.* One third of the existing Senate must accept and elect the person nominated by the Crown within one month, or the Crown must proceed to a fresh nomination. These senators to hold office for life (subject to following provision), and future vacancies in their number to be supplied by similar nomination. To be removable on address of Houses of

* This would give a wide field for selection, while it excludes mere beef-eaters. The Senate and the Governors-General would each prevent the other from obtaining a monopoly of the certificates. The Senate would not certify regarding unfit men, nor would Lords Ellenborough, Hardinge, or Dalhousie.

Parliament. A reasonable retiring pension to be provided after long service, and Senators to be pensioned on attaining the age of seventy years, unless Houses of Parliament address the Crown in their favour.

5. The remaining seats to be filled by election as at present (with the proposed addition of resident fundholders to the constituency) ; the senators to hold office for five years, to go out by rotation, and to be immediately re-eligible, provided that their age at time of re-election does not exceed seventy years.

6. The Senate to elect among themselves six Committees, " Political," " Home and General," " Finance," " Judicial," " Military and Naval," and " Moral and Material Improvement," and every Director to belong to at least one committee ; also to elect a vice-president, who shall be ex-officio chairman of the home and general committee, and four chairmen of the remaining four committees (the president being ex-officio chairman of the political) ; all these offices to be held for five years, and the holders to be re-eligible.

7. The proceedings of the political committee to be, if the president consider it necessary, secret, and orders to be in that case despatched and received without consulting the general Senate. In case of difference of opinion, the president to have the power of acting on his own responsibility after receiving the opinion of the members ; but if a majority of the committee protest, the president must obtain the concurrence and signature of the First Lord of the Treasury and two Secretaries of State.

8. All despatches received from India to be referred to, and all measures to be first discussed in, the committees to whose department they belong. The committees to prepare despatches or drafts of proposed resolutions, which drafts (being other than secret despatches)

shall be ready for the inspection of all Senators the day before a general Senate is held. Committees shall also prepare drafts on such subjects as the President shall order.

9. A general Senate to be held weekly. Each Chairman to produce the drafts which have been submitted for inspection the day before, and the said drafts to be accepted, rejected, or remitted with instructions, with or without comment. Measures proposed in full Senate to be referred for report of committee.

10. The president may either assent at the time, or retain the draft for one week for his consideration, and then may either assent, or veto in the name of the Crown, or may alter the draft for recorded reasons. If the Senate protest against alteration, the president must obtain the signatures of three ministers, as in rule 7.

11. Two to be a quorum of each committee, and eight of the General Senate. Senate to have power to regulate leave of absence, &c., of members, so that the quorum be made up; and provided also that any member absent for more than half the year, or not attending regularly during the other half, is to have no pay or patronage for that year.

12. In the exercise of all patronage, and in making all appointments, the president to have a power of veto as in everything else, but no power of substituting another name; and also to have no power of increasing or inserting grants of money.

13. Either the Crown or the Senate may at any time dismiss any servant at home or abroad; but in case of dismissal of a Governor-General by the Senate without the sanction of the Crown, a concurrent vote of three-fourths of the whole number shall be necessary.

14. Each Director to receive 500*l.* per annum, and a

limited share of patronage to be subsequently proposed. Vice-president to have 1500*l.*, and chairmen of committees 1000*l.*

Supposing the Indian central government to be rendered more efficient, and the business to be sent home in a more advanced stage of digestion than the present crude and unassorted masses of manuscript, the mere mechanical portion of the establishment at the India House might doubtless be very much reduced, and a considerable expense would be saved. But the senators being still numerous, and paid rather as deliberative statesmen than as working officers, much important work, including the greater part of the laborious business, must still be done by the secretaries or examiners. They might be re-distributed to suit the altered constitution of the Senate, and their liberal remuneration would be as now well earned. They would be appointed by the Senate (or the Committees), subject to the veto of the President, in the same way as all other appointments. The President would have a private secretary, and, as chairman of the political committee, the political establishment would be more immediately subject to him.

One question, however, cannot but suggest itself, whether the isolation of an exclusively home service is not a disadvantage—whether, with so large a supply of Indian men of business, many of whom are driven home by the climate while eminently fit for service in a temperate latitude, there might not be some exchange between the Indian and home services—whether great benefit would not result from employing in the India House men of Indian experience, while, on the other hand, there are several appointments in India connected with finance and accounts, the post-office, sea customs, &c., to which the regular course of the civil service does not directly lead, and which might sometimes with advantage be filled by men of business trained in England. Such an arrangement would go a very long way to promote an efficient understanding between the governments in India and at home. At present the evil is just, in a very much enhanced degree, that which would be felt by a governor in India, whose whole staff, secretariat and councillors, had been all their lives exclusively confined to the Calcutta offices, and who had never been in the interior of the country—an evil the partial occurrence of which in particular instances all Indian statesmen loudly deprecate. Yet the Indian government is now carried on in Leadenhall Street with a great staff, of whom I believe that only one individual has ever been in India. This makes it a very close bureaucracy. I doubt whether it is possible for any man to understand any business in which he has never taken an active share from mere paper knowledge ; he can only see things from one point of view ; but especially it must be absolutely impossible that an Englishman, who has never breathed an Asiatic atmosphere, can really comprehend Asiatic manners, Asiatic feelings, Asiatic facts, and Asiatic business. He has at best a sort of reflected and negative knowledge. A man may come to accept certain facts and a certain course of things, and he may do excellent service by abstaining from innovation, and from treading ground beyond his depth, but he cannot get beyond this point. Take, for example, the case of Mill, the historian, who continually falls into blunders which the dullest of Indians could correct. Then why should not Indian experience be made available at home in the executive as well as in the deliberative offices ? Might not a portion of the home duties be amalgamated, as it were, with the Indian service, and the servants be made interchangeable ? Might not a secretary of the East

India House, possessed of all the views of the Home Government, possibly be sent with great advantage as financial minister to the government of India, and might he not return not only the ablest of secretaries, but a practical Indian politician? and might not a distinguished secretary to the government of India fill with great advantage a similar office at home, throw a flood of light into the minds of the Senate, and a few years after, with renovated health, an Anglicised mind, and a thorough possession of the views of and accord with the government at home, be sent to manage an Indian presidency?

I may say, without disrespect to the distinguished men who hold office in the India House, that there must necessarily be, in that establishment generally, a want of the practical knowledge which is necessary to eliminate, understand, and collate the facts stated in various forms and various language in the voluminous papers now sent from the different presidencies in India,—and that some admixture of Indian practical knowledge might be of great use to them.

It also strikes me that great advantage might be derived from digesting, extracting, and converting for publication the marrow of the great mass of facts, arguments, and hidden *Proposed digestion and publication of official information.* talent now scattered through and buried in piles of papers like the nuggets of gold in California or Australia. Very few official documents are in their original state fitted for publication, because they are not written with that view; and it is one thing to write for an official superior, another for the general reader. But there might be a literary establishment at the India House expressly devoted to compiling papers for publication for the benefit both of the Indian services and of that portion of the public who take an interest in the subject. Nothing can be more striking than the want of informa-

E

tion of this kind under a government which has all possible and most minute information in manuscript almost to excess, and the want of the opportunity of knowledge almost justifies the general ignorance which prevails.

The Senate might also with advantage address an annual report to the Crown, giving some general account of its proceedings and views, the whole or part of which the Crown might cause to be published for the benefit of the nation.

I have not yet noticed the Court of Proprietors as The Court of taking a part in affairs beyond the election Proprietors. of Directors. It seems that they exercise little real power, except the important right of vetoing money grants of the Directors; an appropriate and necessary privilege, when the money was theirs, and their interests were directly involved. Under present arrangements this power is no longer necessary to secure the pockets of the proprietors; and the interests of India might be, I should say, sufficiently secured from abuse by the joint responsibility of the Senate and the Ministry, and by a provision for giving publicity to grants of money. It would not, therefore, seem necessary on this account to continue the existence of the Court of Proprietors; but there is another use, which is urged with considerable reason, viz. the advantage of securing a public vent for grievances, and the means of bringing to light and holding up any real abuse of the powers of an oligarchy sitting with closed doors. Parliament has only sufficient interest in the subject when other feelings are brought into play which are certain largely to influence it, and which leave so little confidence in the verdict that it is generally agreed to be better to avoid such discussions. When only the interests of India are concerned the House is counted out. Public meetings, then, of persons *bonâ fide* interested in and having some knowledge of

India, and the opportunity of seeking and giving explanations, might be very useful. But does the Court of Proprietors supply this want? I should say decidedly not. Look at the account of the meetings. What is the attendance? Most miserable. The whole affair is almost monopolised by one or two pertinacious people, who have hobbies which they have long ago ridden to death, yet persist in attempting to galvanise.

To answer the purpose indicated, the meeting must be put on a broader basis. Now, though it would not do to give to Indian servants and residents retired or temporarily at home the power of electing Directors, or any other actual power, I should say that the privilege of talking and expounding their views might, with great advantage, be accorded to them. It is true that at present any one can buy a qualification to talk in the Court of Proprietors; but he cannot buy a respectable audience, with which I think that the following plan would supply him, if he had anything interesting to say. I would propose to substitute for the present quarterly Court of Proprietors a Court of Experts, which should consist not only of all proprietors of 500*l.* stock, but also of all who are or have been in a respectable position in India. Proposed Court of Experts. I would make the qualification as wide as possible. It should include all the servants, or former servants, of the Government, from an ensign upwards; all persons who have ever paid 50*l.* per annum of land revenue, or 50*l.* sea customs, in India; all who have held any considerable offices in the presidency towns : all merchants, planters, &c., of respectability. The servants of the Company are so numerous, that in such a body I do not think that we need fear a democratic majority. I would give to this quarterly Court of Experts the privilege of making presentments of their opinion to the Senate, on which the Senate should be bound to make some deliver-

ance. I do not think that the Indian Government has
any occasion altogether to shun the light, and believe that
it would be much better that those who allege that they
have grievances should have an opportunity of explaining what they want, than that they should be free to abuse
the Government in a general way, without suggesting a
particular remedy. For instance, the Company's government has always been talked at as if it were to blame for
not supplying good and cheap cotton. Let any one who
thinks so propound a plan of improvement in the Court
of Experts; let him be heard and answered. In any
view I am sure that it would be infinitely preferable to
have a fair field for the exposition of grievances in this
country than that the Indian press should propagate un-
contradicted misrepresentations. Freedom is not dangerous or even inconvenient in a free country. How many
monstrous accusations are dissipated by a parliamentary
explanation ? I believe that many horrible things laid
to the charge of the Indian Government would be equally
dissipated in the Court of Experts. This fitting freedom
of speech and explanation would be much more appropriate in this country than in India, the seat of an
absolute and military government, where explanations
cannot be exchanged on equal terms, and where the
government now submits in silence to calumny.*

The particular mode of securing a due qualification in
Patronage.   the young men sent out to serve the Indian
            Government will be most properly dealt

* When I accused the Indian papers of scurrility, I confess that I should
have made some exceptions, and more particularly that very excellent paper
' The Friend of India.' I may also observe that as yet I have committed
myself to no opinion that the Indian press should *not* be free : while I
strongly object to the unmerited abuse and most gross misrepresentation of the
Government which attempted to detect alleged Commissariat frauds, I do
not forget that a gagging law which should protect it might also protect Sir
C. Napier from that truth (in this case as good as fiction) which has so
galled him.

with in connection with the general constitution of the services; but as something must, under any circumstances,
remain matter of patronage, I would here only treat of
the disposal of that patronage, properly so called, bearing in mind, however, that I shall hereafter suggest so
great an enhancement of the qualifications as very materially to diminish the value of the patronage as patronage. All nominations are now, as it were, the private
property of individuals, being divided among the Directors, and each disposing of his share as he thinks fit. It
is desirable in the new arrangements,—first, to be
rid of the patronage as a political difficulty; second, to
provide for the bestowal of appointments in acknow-
ledgment of and reward for public service; and, third, to
open the services more to the general public, inasmuch
as they have hitherto fallen too much into the hands of
particular classes.

The system hitherto pursued, of giving all the patronage to the Directors, has acted well as regards English
politics; and there will be no objection to giving to the
Senate and to each Senator a limited share of patronage.
But we must first provide for the other objects which I
have mentioned.

In regard to rewarding public services by appointments, it is very unfortunate that the
claim has been somewhat ostentatiously
brought forward in the only light in which
it is not tenable; and the case attempted
to be set up has completely broken down, to the injury
of the general cause. It has been alleged that the
officers of the army do not receive a due share of Indian
appointments, and demanded that a fixed share of all
appointments should be set apart for them. It is shown
that, in fact, a very large proportion of appointments are
now given to sons of officers, as every one acquainted

Application of a portion of patronage to reward public services.

with India must well know to be the case, successive
generations filling the services, and there being hardly
an officer with a grown-up family who does not get appointments for some of his sons. But the real question
is, are these appointments given for public services, or
in proportion to public services ? and can the best of the
servants of Government, serving his country in India,
submit his case in a proper quarter, and, without personal interest or importunity, ask for and get an appointment for the son? Very far from it. It is not in the
nature of things under present arrangements that it
should be so, while patronage is divided among individuals. A very large portion of the appointments are
given to the sons of old servants, not, generally speaking, in consideration of their services, but simply and
solely because the same interest and personal or clannish
connection which got the father an appointment gets one
for the son. A man belongs to an Indian family, or he
marries the daughter of an Indian family, or he or his
friends, or his friends' friends, have known in India a
man who becomes a Director. It is by these means that
a large share of appointments are secured to the sons.
But all who have observed different families must well
know that the share of these good things is by no means
in proportion to the merits of the father. Many a distinguished man, who remains at his post in India, has the
greatest difficulty in providing for his sons, and does so
in a way quite inferior to the father's position and claims ;
while many another man of no claims at all, but with
some particular channel to a Director, gets the best appointments, especially if he comes home and sets himself
to sit on the heads of his friends, and makes his friends
sit on the head of the Director. In fact, if a man rests
solely on his public services, where is he to go ? The
evil to be remedied is, not that the Directors are ill-dis-

posed, but that no patronage is retained by the body for public purposes. If the applicant applies to the Court, he is told, We have no doubt of your merits, but the Court have no patronage. If, without personal connection, he applies to an individual Director, he is told, " I admit your claim, but I have several nephews to provide for; I am deeply pledged, and why select me? why not go to any of the other twenty-three Directors?" I by no means say that no appointments are given by individuals from feelings more or less public-spirited, but such cases are certainly the exception ; and when they occur, it is still quite wrong that the public-spirited man should sacrifice his private patronage from public feeling, while he who has no public feeling keeps his. The patronage is not in trust, but in private gift. It is not like a duty of filling a responsible office with a fit person. Any boy is considered fit for a cadet, if he can only get an appointment and pass the prescribed tests ; and there is no obligation, legal or moral, to be guided by the merits of the father. Whoever wants an appointment must beg it from door to door ; and the hardship is chiefly felt by men in India, who have not the same opportunities of doing so that those at home have. Many notable instances might be quoted of the difficulties experienced by men holding the first positions in India ; and though some cases have ended honourably to individual Directors, all show that the system is faulty.

It may then be assumed that there is no public arrangement for rewarding service by appointments. Yet when these appointments are to be given away as patronage, could they be more usefully employed? It is argued that servants are paid for their services. So they are, and this patronage is undoubtedly an additional payment. But it would be taken into consideration as such, and would be a form of payment in no way burdensome to the State, and saving a world of anxiety and trouble to meritorious individuals. I would put it on exactly the same footing as similar appointments in the royal army, in which commissions without purchase are distributed by the Commander-in-Chief, as a great public officer, on public grounds, and with reference to the father's services. I believe that an officer of a certain rank and service in her Majesty's army can depend on obtaining a commission for his son; and it is one of the avowed advantages of remaining in that service that it leads to appointments to Sandhurst, &c. What more graceful and grateful way of rewarding the services of Indian officers, civil and military, from a fund of patronage which must be given away somehow, and in regard to which the great object is to get rid of it without raising political difficulties?

I would propose, then, that one-third of the whole patronage should be reserved to be distributed by the Senate collectively on recorded public grounds as a reward for services in India—that every servant of the Company should have the privilege of making application and stating his claims—that the president and chairmen of committees should, in conclave, select those having the greatest claims, stating their reasons—and that the matter should be finally determined in full Court—the president having in this, as in other matters, a right of veto. The names of the candidates and of the persons selected to be published.

It may be more difficult to satisfy the remaining desideratum of opening the appointments more generally to all classes. At present some appointments certainly find

Question of more general distribution of Indian appointments.

their way into every class; but perhaps the highest classes—those which have been in late times deprived of the large patronage and easy way of providing for their relations and friends afforded by the political abuses which are now so much diminished—these classes, I say, have perhaps not so great a share of Indian appointments as their position in the country, the value of the appointments, and the necessities of the aristocracy, would give them a fair claim to have. For my own part, holding the doctrine that it is by no means undesirable to give to the Ministry some legitimate patronage in exchange for the illegitimate patronage which has been taken from them— and believing that the relation or supporter of a minister, or a peer, or a member of Parliament would make quite as good a cadet as the relation of a Director— and that the President of the Board of Control uses his patronage as well as any Director—I should see no immediate objection to giving—say one-third—of the appointments to the Cabinet Ministers; but then there is the danger that the Governor-General in India might afterwards be subjected to undue pressure on account of the persons so nominated; and I am aware that such a proposition is not likely to meet with favour. If the object would be at all effected by selling commissions in the army, I do not know that there would be any great objection. But I doubt whether the purpose, as concerns the aristocracy at least, would be attained by such an arrangement. That class is not in the present day the best provided with ready money, and the effect might be to bring more Jewish than noble blood into the army. In regard to the civil service, any sale of appointments must be injurious. Here the object must be to make the standard of qualification as high as possible, and to let no man purchase with his money what Lord Ellenborough terms a sort of freehold right in his office. It must be much more of the nature of a contract for the highest class of services strictly rendered and paid according to value, and the appointments should no more be sold than English judgeships.

The nomination of a certain number of Senators would have a good effect in making appointments less dependent on the votes of East India proprietors, and in widening the circle of selection; but except in that way, and by selling some cadetships, I do not know that anything more can be done towards this object, if the great English public officers cannot be trusted with a share for distribution among the class to which they belong.

The patronage not disposed of in the modes already Patronage of suggested should annually be divided, as Senators. now, among the Senators—and I would give the president a quadruple share. The number of the appointments in the individual gift of each Senator will be, however, considerably diminished by these arrangements; and this result, with the diminished value caused by increased qualifications, will remove one great obstacle to the appointment or election of Senators on public grounds.

CHAPTER II.

THE INDIAN GOVERNMENT.

I HAVE alluded to the advantage for *Indian* reasons of conducting the government of India *The name of the* in the name of the Crown. In most cases *Crown.* a name is of little consequence, but sometimes it really carries weight; and I think that the time has certainly arrived when the style and title under which we govern India becomes important, and involves considerable principles of policy. Before giving the reasons for thinking the proposed change desirable, I would observe, as an antecedent argument, that there is no real *primâ facie* objection—that no great harm can result. The name, as I understand it, in no way involves either the principle or any important features of the Home Government of India. India is not in fact governed by any joint-stock company whatever, but the details are conducted by a Board, under the superintendence and orders of the Minister of the Crown. The use of the name of the Company confers no material advantage on the proprietors of East India stock. Whatever be the real constitution of the Home Government, whether it remains what it now is, or whatever Parliament may decide that it in future shall be, we may retain the name of the Company, or substitute that of the Crown, without making one iota of difference in the relative powers of the Crown and the East India Directors, or in the advantages possessed by the proprietors of East India stock. Supposing then that there are other reasons for desiring a change

of name, there can be no reasonable objection on the
ground of English politics or English interests.

On the other hand, the reasons for a change are in
India strong and numerous. The Turkish
leaders early made themselves Emperors;
and the Moguls, like ourselves foreigners, and for no
very long historical period rulers of all India, in
occupying the site of the former empire, assumed
that imperial title which commands a large share of
respect in Asia, and is only claimed by sovereigns of
great empires, or of ancient prescription. They so
well succeeded in establishing themselves in the opinion
of all India as legitimate emperors, that the prescription of their name lasted and retained a very considerable
importance for nearly a hundred years after the decline
of their power, and for half a century after they had
ceased to possess any share whatever of actual sovereignty.
Even to this day the honours formerly bestowed by them
are much prized, and I rather think that the present
shadow of former empire makes some little money by
the titles which he confers. We have succeeded to the
Mogul, as the Mogul succeeded to the Turk, and we
have lately attained such complete dominion in India
as Aurangzebe at the very culminating point of Mogul
power never possessed. But we have never claimed the
imperial rank; we have been content to appear as an
upstart race, commencing by trade and ending by a
strong but unlegitimised dominion. We have dealt as on
equal terms with the inferior feudatories of the Moguls,
and they now yield us obedience, but no reverence.
Yet we too have a sovereign of greater power and
more ancient prescription than the Great Mogul, and as
much reverenced by her subjects. Why then have we
not put our own idol in the place of the Mogul, and
made the subjects of Her Majesty's subjects bow down

Reasons for adopting.

and render allegiance to her? Why have we not installed her as Empress of the Indies, and the legitimate fountain of power and honour? We did not do so at first, nor could we have conveniently done so, but it is both proper and convenient that we should now do so.

In fact, while the substance of the Company is gone, we are still hampered with the name, the humility, and the undignified character of the Company; and the only way of getting out of the false position into a true one is by introducing Her Majesty, and requiring from the natives that respect to the throne which we pay to it ourselves. In these things example is everything, and we can only expect the natives to respect that which *we* respect. The Company assumes not the form or dignity of a sovereign. The Company is abused by European settlers, ridiculed by newspaper editors, treated on the same footing as the rest of Her Majesty's subjects in the law courts—and the name of the Sovereign is never used or heard of. Yet nowhere is the regal dignity so well understood or so much appreciated as by Orientals, and the title once put prominently forward would soon acquire all the strength of prescription.

First, in our relation with native states the name of the Crown would be of the utmost importance. As concerns the native states. It would not only command their respect, but would be the keystone of the whole policy which should now be adopted towards them. If they are to be maintained, it must be as an integral part of the empire, and the same allegiance which they or their more worthy predecessors paid to the Mogul emperor, they should pay to our sovereign. That should be an indispensable condition of our protection and support, and would be readily assented to. Some settlement on a definite footing of the real position, rights, and liabilities of those states is urgently necessary (witness again those terrific Outram Blue-books, all arising out of the indefiniteness of our relations). The Company, having dealt as an equal in name, cannot easily in the same name assume the character and command the respect of a superior. But in the name of the Crown the feudatory chain may be easily and satisfactorily arranged, and, theory being rendered consistent with fact, a system might be formed securing to each chief the power which he ought to have, and defining that which he ought not to have, and in fact has not had ; a subject to which I shall afterwards have occasion more particularly to allude.

Next, in regard to our own subjects, the effect of the imperial name on their respect, and in rendering comprehensible to them the nature and the stability of our rule, would be great. At present the natives appreciate substantial benefits derived from us, but no great name or intelligible principle of government conveys reverence to their imaginations, or light to their understandings. Our honours, our titles, and our condescensions, carry with them none of the weight which attached to the empty honours and magnificent pretensions of the declining Moguls. All this might be easily changed, and a great Oriental government would assume a more than Oriental dignity, and exercise that moral hold on the mind which gives strength among any people, but especially among Asiatics.

As concerns our own native subjects.

Another advantage in the use of the name of the Crown is in dealing with Her Majesty's judicial and other establishments, and with her servants and European subjects in India.

When India was really intrusted to a joint-stock company, it was necessary that representatives of the Crown should have the power judicially to check the proceedings of the Company; but now that the distinction between the British Government and the Company in reality no longer exists, the traditions of ancient jealousy and antagonism kept up by the name, situation, and semblance of a separate and superior source of authority, are noxious and objectionable. It is perfectly clear that the authority under which *As concerns* all different servants of the state, courts *European courts, subjects,* of justice, &c., act, should be assimilated *&c.* throughout India. It would be difficult and would seem absurd at this time to put the establishments heretofore rejoicing in the Royal warrant, and pretensions attached thereto, under an unsubstantial company, and it would be as efficacious and more easy to assimilate by making all to hold office and act in the name of the Crown.

The European settlers have vigorously opposed their subjection to the Company's courts and Company's servants, and asserted their privilege of being judged by Her Majesty's judges. The more free use of the name of the Crown might smooth the way to the inevitable and necessary equalization of justice, and abolition of class privileges, and would put the Government on that footing in its own courts, and in respect to its own servants and subjects, which it is right that it should hold.

An especial advantage which I anticipate from the introduction of the name of the Crown as the source of Indian office and honour is, that it would *On other* facilitate a more free communication and *grounds.* interchange of services between the servants of the state in India and those in other parts of the empire both in the civil and military departments. It would be well that Indian service should be more and more recognized as no longer the exclusive service of an exclusive company, but the service of the state in India; and the status and just consideration of Indian servants would be increased, while they would be less isolated from European knowledge and communication. Much good might follow from a nearer connection between the Queen's and Company's armies.

Having settled then that the government should be "Her Majesty's Government in India," as in any other part of the British dominions, let us proceed to the constitution of that government.

I have before alluded to the necessity of uniting in one great central government the guiding reins of all the different parts of that great empire which is now, in fact, throughout subject to our rule—the essential characteristics of which are identical in every part—the people of which are morally, socially, and politically the same—and into the whole of which the Mahommedan rulers introduced the same system of government. The Mahommedans, commencing from one point, extended their conquests and their system to the extremities. We, commencing at different extremities, have gradually closed in till we have united the whole. Our military system does not very essentially differ in different parts (for our military system we brought with us), but we still retain very radical and important differences in the civil systems of different provinces, because the whole civil structure was new to us, and different individuals, acting apart and experimentally, have followed very different courses. These cannot all be right; and the comparison of so varied experiences ought to enable us to attain everywhere much greater perfection of administration than has been yet exhibited in any single province.

A union of all the powers of an absolute government in one common centralization must lead to much greater executive efficiency than when the parts are disjointed. Decentralization may act well in free constitutions of a more or less republican kind, but never in despotisms. No tyrant is so bad as a petty tyrant. Hence the advantage of a really active and competent central government. We must govern from afar and administer from near, as Louis Napoleon has it. The local governments must have ample power to administer, but they must be guided, directed, and propelled by the central power. The necessity of checking them financially and politically, of preventing them from running wild and upsetting the coach, has long been felt. But we must not only restrain them from doing wrong, we must propel them to do right, and it is in the latter that we have chiefly failed. If I may take a simile from a subject once familiar, now nearly extinct, I should say that Bombay and Madras are, as it were, the most distant horses of the coach which the Governor-General, as coachman, has under his command, heavily bitted, but which he has not a long enough whip properly to reach; so that, while they are prevented from going forward, they have every opportunity of gibbing and going backward. Bombay, in particular, is a most expensive, ill-conditioned possession, which costs a great deal more than it is worth.

Deficiency of present centralization.

The political atmosphere of England not being suited to a strong, prompt, and bold absolute government, it is, as I have formerly argued, necessary to trust the central executive to the Supreme Government in India. So thought Parliament in 1833, and it was imagined that it had sufficiently provided the means for a thorough concentration of power. It must be confessed that the experiment has, in a great degree, failed. The weather has proved unusually tempestuous—the road has been cut up by divers political torrents—the coachman is not yet sufficiently armed—he has exercised but an authority divided with, and much checked by the control of two guards

F

of very different temperaments—the farther horses pull as little as ever—the coach is very much behind time.

It is necessary, however, to be a little more explicit Nature of de-
ficiencies. as to the extent and causes of the failure of the design of 1833.

Parliament then proposed three principal objects :—

First. To vest a complete central administrative power in a Supreme Government, and thus to secure a uniform and efficient administration throughout India.

Second. To secure to the Central Government so complete a control over and management of the imperial finances as should ensure their healthy condition, and prevent one government from spending what another saved.

Third. To obtain through the Central Government and a law commission a complete, uniform, and simple codification of laws for the whole empire.

Have these objects been fulfilled? I fear not. The administrative system has been in practice but little centralised, and rendered little uniform since 1833. In some comparatively minor matters, as sea customs, &c., something has been effected; but, generally speaking, there is almost as great a divergence and separation as ever. In fact, except as regards legislation and the prohibition of expenditure, Bombay and Madras are still much more under the immediate orders of the Court of Directors than under the Supreme Government.

The imperial finances have doubtless been principally deranged by wars; but also as regards the internal finances of the subordinate presidencies the expected advantage does not seem to have been derived. There is no financial improvement in Bombay and Madras. What has been gained in one way they have contrived to get rid of in another; and Bombay is as remarkable as ever for spending more than her income; while at the same time very strong complaints are made by the subordinate presidencies of their inability to spend money for useful purposes.

The legislative failure is the most complete of all. We seem to be no nearer codification than ever. Our laws are more uncertain, insufficient, and unintelligible than before. The way that has been gained by partial and patchwork amendment on the part of the legislature has been more than lost by the accumulation of crude and contradictory precedents, constructions, and other judge-made laws; and the absence of result is really (I can call it by no milder term) disgraceful.

In fairness it must be admitted that the members of the commission have not been altogether idle; but they seem, for the most part, to have worked without reference to the real current necessities of the state, and to have done anything and everything except what they were expected to do and paid for doing. One would think that they had been sent to India to speculate more quietly and at their ease on juridical subjects of English and European interest. They have been much occupied by matters relating to the small local jurisdiction of the presidency courts, and have furnished no end of elaborate reports on "the fusion of law and equity," and I don't know what besides, while, practically, they have done nothing. I hope that their researches may be useful to law reformers in England, but "the fusion of law and equity" can have little interest in a country where those branches of law are not separate,* and do not want fusion; and I fear that from the Governor-General downwards no one in India cares even to read all these valuable reports.

* Except, of course, in the Presidency Courts, which are regulated by English law, and in regard to which such a question will not be determined in India.

From what I have said of the unpractical working of the law commission I must certainly except the Macaulay code. A penal code, though not the *most* necessary or most difficult of the objects proposed, is a highly practical and useful work. Macaulay's code was completed very early in the existence of the commission. It miscarried from attempting too much, and from that time the commission has not advanced one step.

This failure may be traced, in great part, to other causes; but much is also due to the general short-coming of the Supreme Government, as a propelling power in the internal administration of the country.

I shall here, then, sum up what seem to me to have been the causes of the general failure of the Supreme Government, in addition to the impediments resulting from the cumbrousness of the Home Government, to which I have already alluded.

And causes.

First is, no doubt, the unfortunate occurrence of harass-ing wars and political anxieties which have occupied the greater part of the time and attention of successive Governors-General.

Second, the position of the seat of Government, which has caused the Governor-General to be for the most part, and the Commander-in-Chief and head-quarters of the army always, separated from the council, and from all the offices and records of Government; and the climate of which has made the Governors and councillors less healthy in body, and less active in mind, than they would be in a better situation, and has *pro tanto* dimi-nished the value of their appointments and their wish to retain them.

In the position of the seat of Government.

Third, the constitution of the government, the result of which proves to be, that the Governor-General has generally very little *active* assistance from his council in carrying on the administration. He has not only all the power (to which I do not at all object) but also all the labour.

In the constitution of the Government.

Everything seems to fall on him. The council is, in most instances, simply and solely a consultative council; and beyond the duty of warning the Governor-General when he is going wrong, the office of the councillors may be, and most frequently is, nearly a sinecure. In fact, they are paid for merely giving advice, as no councillors ever before were paid for such a duty. In many constitutions we have honorary or slenderly-paid councillors of this kind, who happen to reside at the seat of government; but I doubt whether such a thing is elsewhere known as paying a man on the *active* scale, buying him out and out, body and mind, as it were, and then employing him *passively*, merely to be consulted. In all other governments, whether it be a constitutional monarchy, a despotism, or a republic, persons so entertained on *active* pay are actively employed; acting is combined with advising, on the sound principle that practice is not a disqualification, but the best qualification, for advising; and they are separately the responsible ministers of particular departments, collectively the cabinet council of the chief of the state. But in India things are differently arranged. The highly-paid councillor is but an adviser; and the real ministers of the chief are the secretaries, who may do much of the active work of their respective departments, but are not responsible ministers, and do not hold a distinct position as the initiative heads of those departments. They cannot act as recognised ministers; and a Governor-General who does his duty is supposed to act, not on their responsibility, but on his own, and should (I believe that Lord Dalhousie does) go into everything himself. The consequence is, that the governor must either in an irregular way make the secretaries *de facto* ministers,* or is himself much overworked and unable to attend to many important matters, while the councillors do as little as may be. I do not object to the councillors hitherto appointed as *passive* councillors. They are, for the most part, excellent good men; and if the fire of their energies is somewhat expended, they are not the less sage and sound negative advisers against rash error. But I say that neither is theirs the position to act, nor are they generally the men to overcome that position. They are appointed by the Court of Directors somewhat late in the day, as the reward of long and tried past services. They have generally nothing farther to look to; they have the initiation of nothing; and there is no call, and very little temptation to them, to embroil themselves as the advocates of anything new. They all (almost without exception) merely look on their five years in council as the means of quietly and tranquilly accumulating a considerable sum as the reward of past less liberally paid services. Their only personal care is to preserve their health, to make out their time, and to carry home their savings. They give their conscientious, and generally sound, opinions on the questions submitted to them ; and it is no matter of blame to them that they do no more. But the system is a reason why the Government is less actively efficient.

The Governor-General has been also saddled with the responsibility of the local government of Bengal, which is simply another heavy load placed on the back of an overburdened beast. If his share in the Supreme Govern-

---

* And even in this case, if the Supreme Government were really to govern India, the Home Secretary alone could not possibly be equal to all the interior duties including revenue and justice.

ment is already more than sufficient, it may be supposed that to couple with it another office is altogether fatal to his efficient performance of either duty.

Another great obstacle has been the want of information in regard to Madras and Bombay. While the law commission was in full numbers, there was a Madras and a Bombay servant with the Supreme Government on that duty; but latterly this has not been the case—both councillors and secretaries have been appointed exclusively from Bengal—there has been in the Supreme Government no personal knowledge of the other presidencies, and the Governor-General has had no leisure to visit them. There is a great gulf between the services of the different presidencies. Neither can there be any interchange of appointments, nor is there almost any opportunity of personal intercourse whatever. Abstracts of the proceedings of each government are no doubt received in Calcutta; but there seems to be the greatest possible want of any general or condensed views and explanations of their operations for the benefit of those not technically acquainted with their present system, and with their official language. I cannot find, for instance, that any annual or general reports of the revenue systems of Madras and Bombay, and of such-like matters, anywhere exist. Their local papers are forwarded in masses, according to the old routine; and even in matters which are radically the same as those already understood, a few of their peculiar terms, and some differences of form and of conventional language, are (unexplained) sufficient to puzzle and confuse. I believe that to master their administrative system from these documents, without personal explanation, requires an amount of labour which neither Governor-Generals nor secretaries have ever found time sufficiently to achieve while actively engaged in other duties, and in the comparatively short period during which each individual holds the same office. Now, no sound statesman will make radical alterations till he thoroughly understands the facts as they exist, their bearing and results. This information the Supreme Government generally does not possess; and they have consequently refrained from active interference.

With regard to the divided authority over the local governments of the Supreme Government and Court of Directors, it may perhaps be remarked that, if this is partly the cause, it may also be, in some degree, the consequence, of failure on the part of the former, and that, if the Supreme Government took the duty upon itself, the Court might be willing enough to permit it to do so. But then it must itself have sufficient power. If a question must be referred home in the end, it may just as well be sent direct.

The recapitulation of what has been deficient in the Indian government naturally suggests the remedies. I have already proposed the improvement of the Home Government, and the rendering the Indian Government more free to act without constant reference home. Of Indian remedies the following are the most important. First and Remedies for these deficiencies. Peace. chiefly, peace; and believing, as I still do, that we have reached the natural limits of India; that no danger threatens from within; that the Burmese war is no more a necessary consequence of the possession of India than a war with Greece on the Don Pacifico question would have been a necessary consequence of the possession of England; —believing also that the operations against the frontier tribes beyond the Indus, harassing as they are, constitute at worst but a little war, such as has always existed in those parts, and that the state of Asia beyond the Khyber is not at present menacing; —

believing all this, I think that it is in our own power to keep our Indian empire free from serious war, and to dedicate the energies of the Government and the resources of the state to a career of peaceful improvement. No limits are so strong or so useful as ethnological limits; and when we find ethnology, geography, and historical prescription all uniting to assign the same limits to India, and those the limits of our present empire, we have in Asia the same good fortune which in Europe we alone of European countries possess, and we shall be rash if we overstep the limits so markedly fixed by nature.

Next we must constitute the government in such a way that the executive may be equal to the task thrown upon it; that all the labour and all the responsibility may not be thrown on one overworked Governor-General, perhaps little experienced in Indian affairs. Let him have not passive councillors and irresponsible secretaries, but responsible ministers of departments; let them be so appointed as to secure the greatest present energy; let them be men fitted to be the active ministers of a great empire; the first working men of the day, men who feel a pride in, and the certainty of deriving just credit from, their duties; men rising, and hoping to rise still higher. Make the Governor-General the absolute and undoubted head of the Government, but not in himself *solely* the executive Government. That is what is really wanting. Could any one man, if ever so able and experienced, do all the work of England, or of any great empire under the sun, without the aid of responsible ministers and officers of state, and some division of labour? Yet so it now is in India. Combine the duties, positions, and qualifications of the members of council with those of the secretaries, and

In the constitution of the Government.

you have something near what is required. At present you pay for two sets of officials, and the object is not effected—those who counsel cannot act, and those who act cannot counsel. Responsible ministers will do both. The Governor-General must be disencumbered of the duties of a subordinate government. You must also have a new and efficient law-commission, forming a department of the Government, and the Government must be responsible that the work is not neglected. Means must be taken to secure to the central Government a knowledge of the systems, the circumstances, and the wants of Madras and Bombay. Without fixing any precise rule, it will not be difficult, among the ministers, law-commissioners, judges, and other officers In acquiring information. of the Supreme Government, to have at headquarters persons personally acquainted with those presidencies; the appointments in the central administration being bestowed indiscriminately on all the servants of the state, with reference to personal fitness, and to the necessities of the Government. Some interchange and intercommunication between the servants hitherto employed exclusively in their own presidencies should be established; and when the whole attention of the Governor-General ceases to be occupied by wars, he, and a deputation of the central Government, may, with the aid of steam, in three or four months of the cold weather, make tours of the minor presidencies, returning to their regular duties at head-quarters for the rest of the year.

The heads of the subordinate governments, and of the principal departments in each, should be required to condense all the results of their operations of each year, to explain their systems and principles, and elucidate their working: in short, to supply the methodical and intelligible information which has been hitherto so much wanting. I would especially enforce this system of condensation and explanation in all departments. It has always been too much the fashion in India to substitute masses of crude matter for a graduated system of information, by which each official class should condense for that above it. It is easier to make a clerk copy all the papers of a case than to analyze and explain it.*

Finally, the Supreme Government must be fixed in such a place as will afford a reasonable probability that the Governor-General will not be much detached from his head-quarters by his political and military duties or the necessities of his health, and, to secure the Governor-General, you must also have the Commander-in-Chief and the head-quarters of the army at the same place; for it is quite impossible that the head-quarters of the civil and military administration should be permanently located apart. If the Commander-in-Chief does not come to the Governor-General, the Governor-General must go to the Commander-in-Chief. Political and military considerations must be all-powerful, and it is useless to attempt to make a government efficient if you locate it where the head is likely to be constantly called away. Moreover, as the Governor-General and his ministers must always be but men and exotics, it is a fact that in a tropical climate their health must be most precarious, and that in a situation unfavourable in a sanitary point of view they have been, are, and always will be, drawn away by considerations of climate. If, then, the geography of India admits of posting them in a good climate

In the location of the Government.

---

* I am sorry to see, for instance, that the Agra Sudder Court, which used to submit a report on the proceedings of the judicial department of that government, has lately stated that, finding that the Calcutta Sudder does not do so but only sends up a prescribed form of figured statements, it thinks it expedient to act uniformly, and to do the same; wherefore in future it also will submit no report, comment, or explanations, but only the formal papers.

without causing injury in other respects, we should indisputably obtain a great public gain ; and you could more easily and cheaply command better services of better men than by requiring them to serve in a bad climate. Temporary absences on cold-weather tours for business purposes would do no harm and much good, if you can only be sure of your Governors in the hot weather ; but if the cold weather be spent in looking after a campaign, and the hot weather in the hills looking after the Commander-in-Chief, the politics of the frontier, and the Governor's health, while the head-quarters of the Government are far away, what becomes of the internal administration ?

I think that it will be the easiest arrangement here to give the government as I would propose it, leaving farther comments and explanations to follow.

Summary of proposed Supreme Government.

Constitution of Government.   1. The Supreme Government to consist of the Governor-General and the following responsible advisers :—

Minister of political affairs . . } to be members of a committee
Minister of the interior . . . } of public affairs.
Minister of justice, to be vice-president of a committee of justice.
Minister of revenue . . . } to be members of a committee
Minister of finance . . . . } of resources.
Minister of military and naval affairs } to be members of a committee
The Commander-in-Chief, *ex officio* . } of war.
The governor, deputy or lieutenant governor, of the place where the Supreme Government may assemble.

The above to form the cabinet council of the Governor-General.

Two law commissioners subordinate to the minister of justice, and to be members of the committee of justice.

Four committees (of public affairs, justice, resources,

and war) to be formed, each composed of the Governor-General and members designated above; and the Governor - General may appoint any local governor a member of any committee within his territories. The committee of justice to act as a law commission.

2. The Governor-General and Commander-in-Chief to be appointed by the Senate.* *Appointment and removal.*

The ministers and law commissioners to be appointed by the Governor-General in council, subject to the approval of the Senate, from servants of the Indian Government of ten years' service in India, with exceptions following; and on prospect of a vacancy, such appointments to be made such reasonable time beforehand as may give the Senate an opportunity of exercising the veto before entrance on office.

Exceptions.—i. Competent persons, other than those described, may be specially and exceptionally appointed to these offices by special concurrence of the Governor-General and the Senate, provided that not more than one member of any committee shall be appointed under this exceptional rule.

ii. If the Minister of justice be not appointed under the above exception, then one law commissioner shall be appointed by the Senate, being a person professionally trained to any European system of law or jurisprudence.

All the above officers (including the Governor-General and Commander-in-Chief) to be appointed for five years as a definite limit; but to be re-eligible. To be removable only by the Senate or the Crown.

3. The Government of India to obey the orders of the Senate in all things, but the latter *Position in regard to Senate.* to be interdicted from interfering in the

---

* In this chapter, when speaking of the acts of the Senate, I imply all the conditions and restrictions on those acts provided in the previous chapter. For instance, appointments to these offices must be confirmed by the Crown.

patronage vested in the former. Information of the proceedings, and as far as may be of the intentions, of the Indian Government, and other information, to be transmitted to the Senate, in such form and at such times as they may from time to time direct.

4. The Government of India to be absolute over the local governments, but to be authorised to delegate to them such powers in regard to local legislation, executive functions, and finance, as may seem expedient (under an administrative code to be as speedily as possible drawn up) ; also to prescribe rules for the transmission of information.

Position in regard to local governments.

5. In the Government of India the Governor-General to be absolute, subject only to the obligation of consulting his responsible ministers, and to the conditions hereunto annexed.

Position and power of Governor-General.

6. No order in any department shall be issued by the Governor-General, except through the minister of that department, and till the matter has been considered in the committee of which the minister is a member. The minister shall express his opinion in writing, and his colleagues shall either assent or record separate opinions.

Each minister shall be the responsible head of his department, but shall obey the Governor-General in all things. The Governor-General in Council may from time to time delegate to him the power of acting in minor matters within prescribed limits in his own name and on his own authority. In matters beyond these limits he shall be entitled to present proposals to the Governor-General, on which the latter shall be bound to make a deliverance, *e. g.* "The minister of justice proposes so and so," "The Governor-General consents," or "The Governor-General negatives, or orders so and so ;" and this document shall remain of record in the office.

Position and power of ministers.

The members of each committee shall have access to the offices of the ministers grouped in that committee, and any member may at any time mark any subject for discussion in committee, and there give his opinion.

7. In the political department, when a measure has been discussed in committee, the Governor-General shall then be free to act on his own responsibility, and at his own discretion, *Ultimatum in political department.* with the annexed exception; but in case of difference of opinion between the Governor-General and a majority of the committee, copy of the proceedings shall immediately be sent to the political committee of the Senate.

Exception.—The Governor-General shall not make war with more than 1000 fighting men of all arms beyond the geographical limits of India, and of a political arrondissement for the purposes of military police (to be defined by law), without consulting and receiving the opinion of a secret cabinet council.

8 In all departments other than the political, in the event of a majority of the committee finally differing from the Governor-General, *Power of committees.* they may remit the matter for the consideration of a cabinet council.

9. A cabinet council shall be held periodically or specially. *The council.*

All matters referred to the council under the foregoing rules, including the appointment of members of the Government under rule 2, shall be there discussed, and the opinions of the members shall be recorded.

The Governor-General is authorised to take the opinion of the council on all matters in which he may desire it.

The Governor-General is recommended and enjoined to take the opinion of the council on all radical and highly important subjects, in which public injury is not to be apprehended from such discussion.

The decision of the council shall be determined by vote.

Having received the opinion of the council, the Governor-General may act on his own responsibility, but, acting contrary to that opinion, shall by the first post transmit copies of the proceedings to the Senate.

Ultimate power of Governor-General.

10. Laws, the power of making which has not been delegated to the local governments, shall be made by the Governor-General in council ; the Governor-General having in this as in other matters the power of finally acting on his own responsibility.

Laws.

11. All patronage, other than the appointment of members of the Government, shall be exercised in the department to which each appointment belongs, subject to the same rules as any other act of the Governor-General.

Patronage.

12. In the event of the absence or sickness of any minister, the Governor-General in council may either appoint another person to act for him, or may intrust the duties temporarily to another minister.

Provision for absence or sickness.

13. Three members (including the Governor-General), of whom one shall be a servant of ten years' service in India, shall be necessary to form a quorum of any committee—except in the political department when the Governor-General is absent from head-quarters, in which case the Governor-General and one minister, one of the two being of ten years' service, may form a committee.

Quorums.

Four shall be a quorum of the council.

14. When the Governor-General shall have occasion to be absent from head-quarters, he may take with him such members of the government as he thinks proper. Committees and

Absence from head-quarters, and power of delegation.

councils may be formed either wherever the Governor-General may be, or at head-quarters in the absence of the Governor-General, with his consent; and when formed in the absence of the Governor-General, shall have the same power as if he were present in those things which he may intrust to them.

The Governor-General, *with* (but not without) the consent of the council, may delegate to one or more ministers absent from head-quarters the powers and duties of any other ministers within prescribed limits and localities, provided that the rule in regard to quorums be not transgressed.

15. The Governor-General shall be relieved from the labour of a local government, and also from the charge of the various non-regulation provinces now administered by the Supreme Government. Future acquisitions shall be either annexed to existing local governments, or intrusted to a separate commissioner under the Supreme Government till the mode of their government be determined. *Relief of Governor-General from local details.*

16. The Governor-General to be paid as at present. Each minister to receive per annum 8000*l*.; each law commissioner 5000*l*.; the Commander-in-Chief 10,000*l*. consolidated salary, or, in addition to military pay and allowances, 3000*l*. *Salaries.*

17. In extraordinary cases not sufficiently provided for, the safety of the state is confided to the Governor-General, but he is required to take the earliest opportunity of regularly supplying, or obtaining the supply of, what has been wanting. No inferior shall object to the orders of the Governor-General on the ground of illegality. The head of the government is responsible for his acts to his superiors in England, and not to his inferiors in India. *Provision for extraordinary cases.*

This government, while I am sure that it will be infinitely more efficient, will be much less expensive than that last provided by Parliament, as the following figures will show:—

Expense of proposed government.

By the last arrangement, the yearly cost was, besides the Governor-General—

	£.
5 Councillors, including the Commander-in-Chief, - -	50,000
4 Law Commissioners - - - - - - -	20,800
4 Secretaries to the Supreme Government - - - -	20,800
13 persons - - - - - -	91,600

By proposed arrangement—

	£.
6 Ministers - - - - - - - - -	48,000
Commander-in-Chief - - - - - - -	3,000
2 Law Commissioners - - - - - - -	10,000
9 persons - - - - - -	61,000

Gain—four persons, and 30,600*l.*

It will be seen that although, from the separation of departments, the government proposed by me may at first sight have looked formidable, there is in reality a great diminution of numbers as well as of expense. The undersecretaries and subordinate establishments would be distributed among the ministers without additional expense.

The plan amounts, in fact, simply to this—to raise the political, military, and finance secretaries to the rank of ministers, and, instead of the home secretary and the counsellors, to have three ministers—of the interior, of justice, and of revenue.

I have designated the minister who stands first in my list " Political " in the Indian conventional, rather than in the literal, sense of the word. The recent term " Foreign " is not applicable, because the greater part of his duties are not foreign at all, but connected with the dependent states in the interior of our empire, and which

Explanation of proposals.

Character, duties, &c., of the ministers,

I propose to put on the footing in name as well as in fact of our feudatories. The political minister will be charged with all our relations with these states, and with such diplomatic business with states beyond our frontier as may be inevitable.

The minister of the interior will be charged not only with all general matters not particularly falling within the separate departments of justice and revenue, but especially with education and public works, and the whole great task of the moral and material improvement of the people and the country—subjects of which the superintendence would give ample employment to the ablest of men.

As external and internal affairs most directly affect one another, these two ministers (political and of the interior) will be most appropriately grouped as the Governor-General's committee of public affairs.

The minister of justice will have at present, perhaps, the most important and difficult task of all. He will not only superintend the current administration of his department, but will be the actual and responsible head of the law commission, and to him we *and of the law commission.* shall trust seriously and practically to force through to completion the great system of codification and simplification designed twenty years ago, but never executed. The task of improving our laws can be so fitly intrusted to no one as to him who has the daily opportunity of witnessing from a commanding and unprejudiced position their practical working, while at the same time neither is his time occupied nor is his mind confined by the active exercise of the judicial functions of an existing system. I think that two assistants in the law commission will be an amply sufficient number—more would but embarrass. If the minister be a European jurist, his assistants will be selected from the best of Indian servants; if he be an Indian servant, he must have the assistance of an European jurist.

Hitherto it seems that the legislative member of council is not considered to have any *necessary* connection with the law commission. It would appear that he is paid 10,000*l*. per annum for drafting in a uniform and legal form the acts which the Government of India has from time to time occasion to pass—a very useful and necessary duty, no doubt, but one which might be quite as well performed by any clever young man from a special pleader's office. The councillor, however, having nothing else to do, has generally accepted the office of president of the commission. We have seen how completely he and the commission have failed. A good working minister of justice would manage things very differently. I shall reserve for another place the detail of the objects to be set before, and other particulars regarding, the new law commission. Suffice it here to say, that there is every reason to believe that the objects proposed by the last Act, and not attained, may, if rightly set about, be well effected, in a very moderate time, to the immense advantage of the country and the Government. In addition to the permanent committee of justice, the Governor-General will have it in his power to issue special commissions to natives and others, and to employ them in the compilation of particular codes or rules.

I shall afterwards propose a supreme court of justice for all India in connection with the Supreme Government.

The departments of revenue and finance are too large to be managed in all their details by one man. I would, therefore, have separate ministers; one for revenue, to superintend the sources of supply—the great department of land revenue and the minor sources of income; another for finance, to manage the details of expenditure which now give employment to the financial secretary. And, dependent on one another as are these two duties, the two ministers will unite in a committee of resources.

The minister of military and naval affairs will unite the duties of military councillor and military secretary, and this minister with the Commander-in-Chief will form the Governor-General's committee of war (a term which I use for brevity, meaning, in fact, of military and naval affairs). They will also be members of, and assisted by, a military and naval board.

In superintending and sharing all these various duties the Governor-General will have ample employment.

I have adopted the plan of grouping the members of Government in committees for advice and discussion, because, while for executive action unity of purpose and power is indispensable, counsel and warning are sometimes necessary to all men. *Explanation of plan of committees and council.* We cannot always see our own acts as others see them; and the calm assistance of an able unbiassed mind is most important in matters where the active executive officer may be, in some degree, carried away and prejudiced. On the other hand, the whole council would be inconveniently numerous for the transaction of matters of detail. But for the decision of very important measures or obstinate difference of opinion, a cabinet meeting will ensure the amplest discussion and the soundest advice of able men of all departments viewing a matter from many different positions and in many different lights. The local governor will be one of the most practical and important members of the council.

I think it essentially important that under the new system the *initiation* of the appointment of the ministers, as vacancies from time to *Appointment of ministers, &c.* time occur, should ordinarily be vested in the Governor-General in India—the council having the opportunity of expressing their opinions publicly or privately, and the Senate retaining a veto to prevent abuse. Under the present system the appointment of passive councillors by the Directors is quite unobjectionable, and acts exceedingly well. But in regard to active ministers, it is a natural and necessary sequence of the position of the Home Government that their knowledge and appreciation of merit is considerably behind that of the Governor-General on the spot; and that, though they are well qualified to judge, sooner or later, of the most deserving men, they cannot be depended upon to nominate those of greatest present energy and fitness. To do so, they must have not only the usual official documents, but the reports of surgeons, physicians, and mental philosophers. Because a horse won the Derby last year, you will not without inquiry lay your money on him this year. He may be lame, or sick, or sorry, or a better horse, known only to the jockeys, may be coming into the field. So a man who has done excellent service to the state for thirty years past may not be the fittest to undertake a new and more important office, and the interests of the empire cannot be sacrificed to the deserts of individuals. Every man must take his chance, and be estimated at his market value. You must allow your trainer the Governor-General, and his council of jockeys of departments, to place your men, only taking care that he does not cheat you, and interfering when you suspect that your interests are being jobbed or sold.

What I have just said applies to ordinary nominations of persons selected from the Indian service. But a more difficult and debateable question arises in the exception as to the appointment of other persons from England to fill situations in the Indian Government. Shall such appointments be permitted, and on what terms? I have no doubt that

Admission of unprofessional persons.

the places can and generally will be well supplied from the Indian service; but still it seems to me to be desirable that some extraneous blood should, if possible, be introduced. My reasons for thinking so are as follows:—

I have stated, as one advantage and object of a revised scheme of government, and of conducting the Indian administration in the name of the Crown, that there might then be some degree of interchange between the services of the state in India and those at home and in other parts of the empire. An exclusive and class system of government is, on all hands, considered an evil; and while I believe that there is not in the empire any great class of trained professional civil servants of the state at all to be compared to that possessed by the Indian Government, I also think that that class is, in some respects, cramped in its opportunities of acquiring general information; that it may be, in some degree, *too* professional and Asiatic in its feelings, views, and knowledge; and that some sort of community of knowledge and interchange of duties between the trained professional expertness of public servants employed in India, and the enlarged views and information of those brought up in England, might be, with great advantage, established. I do not think that the Indian service would by any means suffer in its personal interests by such an arrangement, if carried out honestly and in good faith. I have proposed that the best Indian servants should be professionally employed in the home portion of the government of her Majesty's Indian territories, independent of the caprice of popular election; and it is a fact flattering to the merits of the Indian service, that, on the mere ground of the market value of their services, several of its members have been employed, and successfully employed, by her Majesty's Government in some of the most important offices under the Government at home and in the colonies abroad. I hope that the frequency of such instances will much increase on better acquaintance; but recriprocity is the soul alike of commerce and of politics; and if it be possible to introduce with advantage into some Indian offices English statesmen or men of business, the Indian services must, in their turn, sacrifice some personal interests to those of the state. In the end I believe that they will be the gainers by free trade in public duties. The strong line of demarcation which has hitherto been drawn, by which, up to a certain point, the Indian service is exclusively privileged, and from certain high offices it is systematically excluded, should be in some degree relaxed. At present the minor governorships of Madras and Bombay are literally the only ground common to English and Indian servants; the Governors-General, Commanders-in-Chief, and legislative councillors being exclusively English: all the rest exclusively Indian. Now I think that, if we are to have English governors at all, it is of the very highest importance that her Majesty's Government should have some men at their command who have not only their personal confidence, but already know something of India and Indian affairs; that a new Governor-General should not necessarily commence the acquisition of the very rudiments of Indian knowledge *after* his appointment; that it should be possible to send a rising man to India in a secondary post in the first instance, where, performing a special duty, for which he has special qualifications, he might acquire a general knowledge of the country and the people, and of the general bearing of all departments. I also think it but fair and reasonable that the best Indian servants should not be excluded by rule from the very highest appointments, and would open everything to their honest ambition, especially when, by service or residence at home, they become personally known to her Majesty's advisers. I would then arrange that between men rising in England who have seen service in India, and men who have risen in India employed at home, a class of statesmen should be formed, common to the mother-country and her great dependency—a connecting link between them—who would introduce into England some knowledge of, and interest in, Indian affairs, and into India some English progress; and that Governors should be appointed from this class: so that, on the one hand, the English politicians sent to India may possess competent knowledge and skill, and, on the other, the highest appointments may be open to the best of those Indian servants who may engraft European progress on Indian experience.

Governors-General have complained of the want of the assistance of English minds in their councils. That assistance would be supplied to them by one or two English ministers, and the possession of such assistance would remove one great obstacle to the promotion of the best Indian professional men.

Altogether, then, I think I may assume that some such arrangement as I have suggested is desirable, if practicable and secured against abuse. Let us see how it can be carried out.

I propose to admit the special appointment of non-Indian persons to the office of minister, *Cases in which* provided that there shall not be more than *such appointments may be* one such person (exclusive of the Governor- *permitted.* General) in any one committee, and therefore no order can be issued without the advice of one or more ministers of local Indian training; such a minister being (I think it will be said with good reason) an essential to form a quorum of each committee. If the Governor-General be a statesman of English education, the political minister must, no doubt, be an Indian officer, both as possessing the necessary knowledge of the natives and of their language, and because, in cases of emergency, the Governor-General and political minister may, on deputation, act alone separate from the council, and the presence of one Indian officer is required to make a quorum of committee. But were the Governor-General, either by previous service or by long tenure of that office, to be himself qualified as Indian, it is not impossible that a rising man might be sent from England, and trained for a future Governor-General in the office of political minister. As to the ministry of the interior, whoever may be Governor-General, it seems not only possible but probable that an able Englishman might sometimes be of the greatest use in superintending plans of education and material improvement, as well as the general discipline of the interior government, purely professional matters (justice, revenue, &c.) being excluded from his department. He would be of much personal assistance to the Governor-General, and not the less so from being free from personal connection in India. Such an appointment might, therefore, be on some occasions quite justifiable.

It is not likely that an English minister of revenue would ever be appointed, because the requisite knowledge of that branch is only acquired by long personal experience, and it is a department in which the Indian service supplies a great abundance of most able and admirable men. But it is quite possible (as I have, in a previous chapter, suggested) that the Senate might wish to send out, as financial minister, on a particular occasion, and with a particular object, a home servant, fully acquainted with their views of finance, and thoroughly practised in its details by India House experience : the subject being one which depends less on locality than any other. The Commander-in-Chief being an officer of the English army, the minister of military and naval affairs must, of necessity, be an Indian officer (to constitute a legal committee), and, of course, would be so on many other grounds. But, an Indian officer commanding the army, it is *possible* that there should be an English military minister.

A mere legal councillor, to draw up the form of Acts, will no longer be necessary—the law-commission will do that; and the ministry of·justice will certainly not be an appointment which can be bestowed on any mere English lawyer. I mean—and I say it, without any disrespect —that such gentlemen, for instance, as are usually appointed to offices in the Indian supreme courts, would not be fitted for the appointment which I am discussing. But one can well conceive a case in which an accomplished European professional jurist, uniting the technical qualifications of a lawyer with the energy and broad views of a statesman, would fill the office with great advantage, being in himself the soul both of the executive administration of justice and of the professional undertaking of the law commission. One can imagine, for instance, Lord Brougham to have made an excellent Indian minister of justice. If we could obtain such a man we might have everything codified in one quarter of the time that the old law commission have consumed in their reports on the fusion of law and equity, and similar subjects. At the same time, unless such a man should be found, it is not indispensably necessary that the minister of justice should be a professional lawyer in the strict sense of the word; it is enough if he is accustomed to view and superintend the working of laws, and the professional commissioners would supply the rest (though, of course, it would be better if the two qualifications should be found united). Either an Indian

officer of enlarged views and some judicial experience,
or say a first-rate under-secretary of the Home Department (who must become, I believe, a kind of *quasi*
lawyer), might be appointed with advantage, selection
being made of the most fit person, Indian or English;
and with one European and one Indian professional commissioner he might carry through the required codes.

It will be observed, however, that I propose to make
every appointment of a non-Indian person to the office
of minister a special and exceptional case. The great
object is to insure against abuse. When the nomination to an appointment is confined to the limit of an
active profession, there is, as I have before argued,
comparatively little chance of abuse, because the candidates, their history and qualifications, are well known,
and a united profession is strong to expose and decry
any gross abuse of its interests. But it is different when
your choice is in no way limited; when there is no
professional standard by which to judge the candidates;
and when the temptation to serve an unprofessional
friend is so much greater than in the case of hiring
a professional man in the professional labour-market.
I have no doubt that all these appointments might be
well filled from the Indian service, and that, nominated
by the Governor-General and approved by the Senate,
they *would* generally be well filled in this way. It is
only when in special cases it seems that a particular
office might be *better* filled by going beyond the limits of
the profession, that an exception should be made; and
I would secure this exception against abuse by the provision that the Governor-General and the Senate should,
by previous correspondence, concur in the propriety of
appointing a particular person. It would be open to
either party, in anticipation of a vacancy, to make a
proposal to the other. If the required concurrence could

not be obtained, the vacancy would be filled up from the profession under the ordinary rule. We may be pretty sure that the Senate and the Governor-General will not concur in the appointment of an unfit man when so easy and satisfactory an alternative is before them.

I have made no special provision for the appointment of a certain number of members of the Government from each presidency, for reasons to which I have before alluded, and because I hope to see established a more intimate connection between the services. I expect that the Supreme Government would, under the new system, become well and personally acquainted with the affairs of all the presidencies, and that the fittest persons would be selected for the offices of the central Government from all India, reference, of course, being had to the particular requirements of the Government at the particular time, and it being probably so arranged that there should be at head-quarters, in some capacity, some person personally acquainted with the affairs of each part of India, to whom reference could be made for petty explanations, dependent on mere local knowledge. In the law commission, too, I have thought it unnecessary to burden a body intended to act with numbers only fitted to deliberate by specially providing a member from each presidency. The old commission must at least have collected a mass of information. If more is required, résumés of existing laws or customs might be well and speedily obtained from the local governments ; and I have supposed the presence at head-quarters of experienced officers from different parts of India, whom the law commission, as well as the Government, might at any time consult. Besides, at any rate, the penal code, which has so long occupied the old commission, has nothing whatever local about it ; and, in

most things, the less local are our simple general laws
the better. It is only when we come to codify the
unwritten civil customs of places and classes that we
become local or rather personal. Mere local regulations
I would leave to the local governments.

I propose to appoint all the great officers of Govern-
Term of appoint- ment, distinctly and definitely, for five
ment. years, supposing them to remain so long
willing and able to serve efficiently. But I would make
them re-eligible, and would by no means desire to
consider five years the practical limit of their term of
office; far from it. On the general principle, that in
the public service we must look not to individual
deserts, but simply to the market value of the services
available, I would never propose to displace a qualified
minister (like a member of council under the present
system) because he had had a fair share of the sweets
of office, and in order that another may have his turn.
Experience is an advantage; wear and tear of body and
mind a disadvantage—and when a man's term is out, I
would simply consider whether the old man or the best
new man to be found is likely to do the best future service. Those rare good men who seem to be occasionally
sent by Providence for the performance of particular
tasks are not so often found that we can afford to lose
them when they occur; and especially in India (it is the
great misfortune of the Government of that country)
it is difficult to retain them so long as we could wish. A
good man should be kept as long as he lasts and will
stay, and should be cherished as the apple of the state's
eye; his health cared for; his personal feelings regarded;
his sons, if well fitted, employed by the Government
without wearing personal solicitation. It is a great deal
too much the fashion in India to work a willing horse to
death. The principle seems similar to that in the

southern slave States: work a man while he lasts; use him up; and then take your chance of getting another. Many a man is exhausted, or retires, who, well cared for, would have lasted much longer; and I think it a great advantage, if, by the division of labour which I have proposed, as well as by the regard to climate in locating the government, which I shall shortly propose, by the mode of distributing patronage suggested in a former chapter, and in other ways, the services of the best men may be secured for longer periods than at present. On the other hand, many men placed in high office without becoming so incompetent as to be ejected on recorded grounds, disappoint previous expectation. Time, tear, and climate, tell on all men; and it is every way desirable that at certain reasonable intervals an office should again be at the unfettered disposal of the Government. It is therefore that not only in practice but in law I would make a new nomination necessary at the end of five years. And then, if the outgoing man be most fit, let him be re-appointed for another term. If such a man as Lord Dalhousie will remain in India he is now doubly valuable after the experience of five years. Why, then, should he be under a sort of prescriptive obligation to resign, and merely asked to stay from year to year? Why should he not be formally re-appointed? I would apply this principle to all the ministers and law commissioners, and shall afterwards have occasion to suggest it in regard to other appointments. At present the Home Government can continue a man in his appointment; but after the usual five years it is a precarious, uncertain, and temporary tenure, very different from a fresh appointment.

In certain cases it is quite necessary that there should be a power of removing from office, by special order, within the allotted term, but this power must, under any circumstances, rest with the Government at home.

That the government of India should be in all things subordinate to the Home Government, and that it should be absolute over the local governments, are essential parts of the scheme of administration. But we may hope that the Indian Government will be permitted the fullest scope to initiate and act, and that the Home Government will for the most part confine itself to supervision and control. To permit the interference of the Senate in the patronage of the Governor-General would defeat the object with which the partition of patronage has been proposed, and it is therefore, as now, prohibited. It is to be hoped that the form of transmitting information will be vastly improved, and that the Home Government will be much better informed of all that is passing in India with a very much smaller expenditure of labour, paper, and ink. It is impossible to fix by rule the particular matters in which the Indian Government must inform the Home Government *before* acting—that must be left, to a certain extent, discretionary ; but I would make it an invariable rule, that, having announced its intentions, and received in a reasonable time no orders to the contrary, it shall be perfectly free to act. The Governor-General should send home an annual budget, but should not be restricted in comparatively small items of expenditure.

To require every local regulation of the subordinate governments to pass the Supreme Government in the form of a law (and it is at present by no means clear what acts are regulated by law, and what require no laws) is a useless hindrance of business ; and it is every way expedient that it should be permitted to the Central Government to delegate to its subordinates the power of declaring certain rules (whether they be called laws or regulations) within their own limits. A check on the expenditure of the subordinate governments is very necessary; but it may be intrusted to the Supreme Government to define the mode in which it is to be exercised, and the degree of licence to be permitted.

That the Governor-General should have the power of acting in all things on his own will and responsibility, when he chooses so to do, is inevitably necessary for the efficiency of an absolute despotism ruling over a conquered country, and to secure the safety of the state. It would never do in a great crisis to admit the possibility of legal and constitutional difficulties. Right or wrong, the Governor-General must for the time do as he will, and answer for his conduct afterwards. At the same time, the obligation of consulting and receiving the recorded opinion of efficient and responsible advisers is a much greater check on abuse or inconsiderateness than any direct limitation which could be put on his power; and I have tried to propose a plan by which due counsel may be secured without the delay, discordance, and other evils attending too great multiplicity of opinions.

Powers of the Governor-General.

If the Governor-General and minister of a department are agreed on a subject, and the other member or members of the committee do not object, there is no need of farther reference. If a difference of opinion is recorded, the Governor-General must consider it well, as, in case of his proving to be wrong, it stands for a memorial against him; and in the event of the difference being maintained on both sides, a reference to the council is every way reasonable.

Mode of conducting business.

Many reasons will suggest themselves why in matters belonging purely to the political department the matter should not necessarily go beyond the committee.

Political department.

H

I do not think that injury can result from the exceptional rule which I have introduced in the

Exception to power of political committee.

political department, and it may save us from future parallels to the Affghan war. The delay in great and distant operations caused by consulting the council will hardly be perceptible, and is in no way to be weighed against the danger of a rash and ambitious or a weak Governor-General involving us in great difficulties. Parliamentary prohibitions of conquest were useless till we reached the natural limits of India; but having reached those limits, we must stop, or we find again no natural limits short of the limits of Asia—and Asia might not pay. India being geographically almost as much isolated from Asia as Britain is from Europe, it is almost as desirable to restrain the too great disposition of rulers to make and meddle in matters with which they have no concern. In addition to the limits of India, I would give the Governor-General power within such a line of ordinary operations (to be geographically defined) as should enable him to act against and chastise frontier tribes and robber enemies, and to secure his external defences; but any operation beyond these limits must be extraordinary, and I only wish it were possible without political danger still farther to curb the power of the Indian Government to go to war beyond its own boundary.

While it is only in exceptional cases that the Governor-

Use of the council.

General is under obligation to consult his cabinet council, it is to be expected that, under the voluntary and recommendatory clauses, that body will be his advisers on almost all broad and important questions, and in a body so constituted there cannot be wanting the best and soundest advice.

In the exercise of the Governor-General's power, I doubt whether a distinction can well be drawn between the laws of an absolute government and any other act: between the power of making laws and the power of acting independent of laws. Such a distinction might lead to the dispute on legal grounds of the acts of the Governor-General. It is enough that the Home Government can at any time order the repeal of improper laws.

Governor-General's power of legislation.

The rule by which patronage is exercised in the department to which each appointment belongs does not stand in need of comment. Each class of officers, political, revenue, or judicial, will be appointed by the Governor-General in consultation with the minister of the department; and general patronage, not belonging to separate departments, or belonging to several departments combined, will pass through the ministry of the interior, the ordinary executive representation of Government being included in this latter class of appointments.

Patronage.

I have already alluded to the principle on which the committees are formed; and as three persons are essential to that principle, and the Governor-General has the power to supply the place, or provide for the functions, of absent ministers, no inconvenience can arise from requiring a quorum of three; which will always be available for any committee, when any three members of the Government are present. In political matters it may however be sometimes necessary that the Governor-General should have every facility of moving and acting uncramped by too much restriction, and I have therefore provided that in this exceptional case two (the Governor-General and one minister) shall be a quorum. The council consisting of nine members, four is a small quorum, and will be always available at head-quarters. I have fixed it so low, that business may not be stopped by any possible contingency.

Quorum of committees and council.

The only restriction which I have placed on the
Single restriction on power of Governor-General. absolute power of the Governor is that which limits his power of acting separate from and without the advice of his ordinary ministers to cases in which the council shall consent to his doing so, and then makes it obligatory on him to take with him at least one minister as his responsible adviser, to whom the powers of other ministers would be delegated. Political difficulty cannot result from this Power of delegation. rule, because on an emergency, taking with him the political minister, the Governor-General and minister constitute a committee all-powerful in political affairs, with the salutary exception already noticed. In other matters of interior administration, it may be presumed that the council will consent to all reasonable delegation of power to facilitate local arrangements; and under this rule the Governor-General, one minister, and the local governor, may with the consent of the council constitute a committee on any subject, at any place ; or with two ministers the travelling government will be in itself sufficiently complete. If the Governor-General when absent from his council differ from his advisers (including the local governor, whom he may at any time call in) on matters other than political, it is only proper that the matter should be delayed and referred to the council for their opinion.

The Government being properly located, we may expect that prolonged delegation will be the exception, and not the rule : but temporary delegation for other purposes than war and climate will be more frequent than at present, and most useful.

The salary which I have assigned to the ministers is Salaries. adequate, but, considering the importance of the duties, and the enhanced value of European labour in India, by no means large. It may, perhaps, be inexpedient to pay a man too high when you want him to work. Both men and animals when over fed get lazy ; you must rather feed them with liberal moderation, their labour considered, and see that they are well treated, stabled, and groomed. At present, members of council have so little to do, and so much to get, that they are not at all in working condition. A minister will work, and hope to rise still higher.

It will be found that the provision for relieving the Governor-General from local details is quite necessary to his efficiency as head of the Supreme Government.

The last article provides for the extraordinary exercise of power by the Governor-General in cases not provided for (of which he must be the judge), and negatives all right of inferior servants to refuse compliance on any ground. *Provision for extraordinary cases.*

For instance, if, the Governor-General being absent on a political emergency, the political minister were to die, and the Governor-General to be left alone, he must act alone. All extraordinary cases cannot be provided for, and you must trust something to a man in the position of the Governor-General.

Before leaving the constitution of the Supreme Government, it may be well here, once for all, to notice the question, whether it is possible to give the natives any share in the govern- *Question of share of natives in the government.* ment of India, or to prepare them in any way for freedom. I might have commenced by stating what I have all along assumed and hold as beyond all question, that the idea of giving them any actual power is altogether chimerical and impossible. Our government must be the purest despotism. We have the best securities in our own constitution that the Englishman who represents this country as supreme ruler of India will act to the best of his power for the benefit of the people, without local connection or prejudice, without the obstacles to executive efficiency, and the danger of the tyranny of a dominant majority or minority, incident to all free constitutions; and also without the corruption and tyranny usually incident to despotisms. This is a great advantage; and I doubt whether it is either desirable or possible to alter it. Even if it were desirable, I believe that political freedom may be indigenous, but cannot be cultivated to advantage. Unless you have an indigenous national aptitude for political freedom, and a prescription deeply rooted in the national mind, freedom is but the freedom from all rule, and another name for anarchy. These conditions are not found in India, where there is not even a united nation. They may exist among certain classes, but not in the population in general. If, then, the advantage of our rule should ever be disputed, it could only be a question between the advantage of a foreign and a native despotism; the one being pure and expensive, the other cheap and probably corrupt. While, therefore, everything should be done to elevate the natives socially and individually, I see no object in attempting their political elevation beyond the limits of small municipalities.

But I can see the very greatest advantage in availing ourselves to the utmost of individual native knowledge and intelligence, as a guide and aid in administering the affairs of a government in which they are interested, and of a people whom they must understand better than we do. There are natives whom I believe to be more qualified, personally, and especially from their position, to give a valuable opinion on the effect of administrative measures and the real working of our system than almost any European. We might at the same time enlist the advice and assistance of such men, and confer on them an honorary distinction, flowing from an avowedly imperial source, which they would highly appreciate.

This brings me to the suggestion of a native consultative council (the proposal that they should have votes in a legislative council being out of the question). To such a council assembling ordinarily for personal discussion there is one positive and one negative objection. The first is, that such an assembly must necessarily be almost entirely composed of natives resident at the seats of the supreme and local governments (supposing the latter also to have consultative councils). But the natives of the present presidency towns are (with a few brilliant exceptions) the worst class whom we could consult: the most Europeanised; the most denativised; the most likely to be influenced by personal interest and intrigue; the least acquainted with what is going on in the country; the most given to call themselves " the natives;" the least in any way representing that class of her Majesty's subjects. To trust to them alone, as exponents of the feelings of " the natives," is most injurious.

The negative objection is, that I doubt the possibility of getting natives to talk freely on doubtful points in a large, and, so far, public assembly.

On matters in which an unanimous opinion prevailed the assent of a respectably-constituted native assembly would carry weight with it; and a dissent would, if the government had been strangely blind to native opinion, probably open its eyes. But practical information and advice on difficult and disputable points is only to be obtained from natives by private conversation, and tested by comparison of arguments.

I would propose that some distinction, corresponding to our rank and office of privy councillor, should be conferred, in the name _Proposed native privy council._

of the Crown, on natives of talent and distinction throughout the country, both on our own immediate subjects and on the feudatories of the empire. Perhaps among this latter class would be found some of the best advisers regarding our internal administration, because they alone are in a sufficiently independent position to give impartial opinions. The opinion of a man placed in such a position as the Nawab of Rampore seems to me especially valuable. This privy council, then, I would not ordinarily assemble as a body, or would do so only for nominal purposes, just like the English privy council; but I would give to privy councillors the privilege of addressing written memorials to Government on public matters, and would enjoin on the Governor-General and Governors to consult by circular, on all subjects on which they may think native opinions desirable, all or a portion of the privy councillors, and on special occasions to appoint a time and place of meeting, where all interested in the discussion of a particular measure should be invited, if it so please them, to attend and expound their views. The opinions of privy councillors, being collated and examined, should be recorded in the proceedings of government, with the reasons for or against acting on the advice given, and should be submitted, in a condensed form, for the information of the Home Government. The Governor-General might also summon particular privy councillors to particular cabinet councils, where their opinions should be recorded, but they should have no votes.

Some such arrangement seems to me to be the proper medium between a Quixotic advocacy of native political rights and a foolish neglect of native intelligence and opinion.

The advantages of privately consulting individual natives are obvious, but cannot be reduced to rule.

An important question remains : where shall the Supreme Government be permanently located ? I have already adverted to some of the *necessary* conditions of good government which involve this question, and shall here sum up the various considerations of necessity and prudence which should guide us in fixing a place as the seat of our government and capital of our empire.

Location of the Supreme Government.

It is desirable that the place should be as central* as possible to the different parts of the empire, and the nearer to England *pro tanto* the better.

Objects proposed.

It is necessary that it should be so situated that it shall be the actual and usual residence of the Governor - General, and the permanent head-quarters of the army ; and to secure these objects it is not only desirable, but necessary, that it should be within reach of those vital political and military affairs, duties, and apprehensions in which the Governor-General and Commander-in-Chief must always be personally engaged.

It is necessary that the seat of government should be so placed, fortified, and protected, that, in the possible event of either internal disturbances or frontier invasion, it should run no risk of falling by any sudden *coup* into the hands of rebels or enemies.

It is extremely desirable that it should be in a climate suitable to European health and energy, in order to secure both the uninterrupted presence and long-continued service of the members of the Government, and their vigorous and zealous performance of their duties ; and it will be a most important end of such a situation that we may make it not only a capital, but also a colony.

It is desirable that the seat of the Supreme Govern-

* I mention this consideration first, rather as that which first occurs than as attributing the first importance to its exact geographical fulfilment.

ment should also be the head-quarters of one of the subordinate governments, and that, if possible, it should be the most important and the best of those governments, the most favourable specimen of our administration, and the best model on which to form the ideas of the English members of the Supreme Government, and on the experience of which to improve the others.

It is desirable that it should be among the finest people in India—those most extensively employed by us, and whom it is most important to attach to us.

Finally, the expense of a transfer must be taken into consideration.

If there were any city pre-eminently the capital of India, or having any claim whatever to that character, it might be natural and desirable to consider first the possibility of making that city the seat of government; but there is, in fact, no such city. Delhi and Agra have ancient prescription in their favour, but that is hardly sufficient, unless it can be shown that the causes which gave them ancient pre-eminence still exist.

Calcutta is still the nominal seat of government,
Supposed *primâ facie* claim of Calcutta.
but there can be no greater mistake than to suppose that, as a city, it has any claim to be a political capital of India ; it is the undoubted commercial capital of Bengal, but nothing more. I do not know that there is any good census of the great towns, but at any rate Calcutta is, even in population, in no way very pre-eminent, and is only one of some half-dozen of the most populous places in India. It has no doubt a larger commerce than any other place, but it is a city of recent origin, and exclusively commercial. It contains no other native aristocracy than the aristocracy of commerce, and has nothing political about it. Now, whatever England may be, the empire of India is not (I will make bold to say) pre-emi-

nently commercial, and there is no reason for regarding commerce alone more than any other great branch of industry. There is no stronger *primâ facie* ground for fixing the seat of the government of India at the most important seaport, than there would be for fixing the government of France at the chief port of that empire. Even the prescription which Calcutta had in some degree acquired while yet our empire in India was only partial, it has quite lost, from the practical fact that for the last twenty years it has not been the actual or usual seat of the Supreme Governor and chief power of the state. With respect to the European residents, I believe that it would positively be a very considerable advantage to relieve a man in so great a situation as that of the Governor-General from the multitude of petty and local business which besets him in such a town in the midst of such a population, and which may with great advantage be left to the local governor.

Denying, then, that Calcutta has any *primâ facie* claim, we must consider it on its merits, and let us see how far it fulfils the required conditions. It will be found that it is singularly ill-adapted to meet them.

First, then, it certainly is not central, and, moreover, it is farther from England than any other important place, and the postal communication is considerably longer. We may assume (for argument) that, coming round the Cape, we commenced our empire at Calcutta, but on that very account it is an extremity, and, the route of communication being now reversed, it is actually the farthest extremity. Even with all the advantages of communication with Affghanistan, the Mahommedan conquerors of India never fixed their seat of empire at Peshawar. They advanced at once to the old Hindoo capital at Delhi, and when their empire extended moved it down to Agra.

Examination of actual fitness of Calcutta.

Secondly, experience has proved that Calcutta is not,
and is never likely to be, the place of

permanent and uninterrupted residence of the Governor-General and Commander-in-Chief. Error may arise from the argument in favour of Calcutta which has been drawn just at present from the Burmese war, and the fact that the Governor-General has been called down to Calcutta to superintend that operation. But I maintain that a Burmese war is the exception, and not the rule; and that the Governor-General has merely been temporarily called from affairs of more permanent importance to look to a local accident. Wherever he is located, such necessities may arise, and, residing at head-quarters as the rule, he may without inconvenience make such temporary expeditions as the exception. Once in twenty or thirty years you may go to war with the Burmese, or Bornese, or Madagascarese, and send troops over the seas to promote your commercial interests and vindicate the honour of the national flag, but you would not in the last-supposed case (of war with Madagascar), because the Governor-General goes to Bombay to superintend the despatch of an expedition, on that account fix the Supreme Government permanently at Bombay. The Burmese war is not necessary or vital. Since the last war there has been no apprehension of danger to India, or to any part of it, from the Burmese. The mountainous country between Bengal and Burmah is a sufficient natural boundary. The Burmese have nothing to do with India, and no connection with Indians. You cannot even find a land route to march troops against them, and if you *will* go to war with them it must be by the aid of your ships. Neither have any non-maritime rulers of India attempted to conquer Burmah, nor are the Burmese really formidable or dangerous to India. Bengal is really quite secure from serious invasion from the east.

It is very different on the real frontier of India. From the north-west frontier conquering hordes have many times issued and many times conquered the country. All great movements in Asia have led to the entrance into India, from that quarter, of nations or armies. Its politics are of vital and constant importance. The north of India, the Hindostan of the natives, has always been inhabited by dominant and warlike peoples; *there* has always been the seat of former empire—*there* is now the nursery of our armies and the seat of our military strength. Calcutta is the point most remote from the frontier—far distant from Hindostan, and isolated from the body of our troops and the centres of our military power. It is not even conveniently situated for the political supervision of the chief native states within India. What follows? Whenever there is anything anxious in the state of frontier, or even internal, politics—whenever there is war or prospect of war (other than maritime and voluntary war)—and whenever there is any important business connected with the army—on all these occasions the Governor-General has been, and always will be, absent from Calcutta—not on occasional cold-weather trips, but habitually, and for years together. He has been in the habit of spending the cold weather in camp, the hot weather at Simla. The Commander-in-Chief has gone further; he has entirely ceased to make any pretence of ever going near Calcutta. And permanent absence of Commander-in-Chief and staff. I believe that, except to take the oath on his arrival, he has literally never sat in council for the last fourteen or fifteen years. Those then who advocate making Calcutta the head-quarters of the government must distinctly make up their minds whether they are also prepared either to fix the Commander-in-

Chief and his staff permanently there apart from the army, or permanently to dissever the head-quarters of civil and military government. That dilemma is inevitable, and is to my mind alone fatal to the *possibility* of making Calcutta the permanent seat of government in the present condition of the empire and position of the army.

We now come to the question of fortification and protection. It is undoubtedly quite necessary that the seat of government should be secured against accidents, and it is very undesirable that it should be placed so near the frontier that the first battle with invaders should be fought under its walls, and the capital be the first trophy of their success. But we are not on this account to go to the other extreme, and to fix the capital, not in the heart, but in the remotest extremity of the empire. If, commencing with a fishing village, we have acquired a great empire, it is an excess of prudence to look forward to the time when, the tide having not only turned, but completely ebbed, we are again reduced to the point where we commenced. When we lose our empire, and are reduced to a corner of a province, it will then be time enough to return to our provincial capital; and when our armies are finally beaten in the field—when even our fortified positions are insecure—when it is necessary to abandon the heart of the country, and our thoughts are turned to our ships, our name and dignity will not stand so high as to suffer much further from the necessity of transferring the remnant of our power from the imperial capital to the fort at Calcutta. I admit that we must render it impossible that any sudden *émeute* or any temporary and reparable reverse of our arms should make the seat of government no longer tenable; but I deny that it is necessary in the plenitude of our power,

Question of fortification and protection.

and in spite of every inconvenience, to keep the seat
of government at that spot which, when reduced to
the very lowest extremity, we shall in the very last
gasp and article of our power the last abandon. We
should be in the centre and present stronghold of our
strength.

Calcutta is certainly far enough from external invasion.
Denuded of troops as is Bengal, it is at least as liable to
the approach of sudden internal disturbers as any other
of our great cities; and I am not strategist enough to
know whether the vicinity of the fort would necessarily
save the city from plunder. But granting this to be the
case, we merely admit that one necessary condition is
fulfilled by Calcutta—not that it alone can fulfil that
condition.

But it is said that we are a maritime people, and therefore we should have a maritime capital;   Naval protec-
and here lies the fallacy which has had such   tion.
force. It is true that England is a maritime nation, and
that India is protected from the seabord side by the
marine of England. But our empire in India is not naval.
It is, on the contrary, essentially military. The very fact
of the naval superiority of England makes the Indian
marine of comparatively little consequence. We shall
never (it is to be hoped) be attacked in India by sea;
but many powers have looked to attack us by land, and it
is to our army that we must trust. It is true that, if we
are ever reduced to the fort at Calcutta, a fleet might
throw in supplies there, and enable us to hold out the
longer; but I have already argued that our last point of
possession and defence in adversity is not necessarily the
capital of our prosperity. You would not fix the capital
of Britain in Scotland, because when Louis Napoleon
conquers England you may hold out in Scotland.

But it is still argued, "the supplies of our army come

from the sea." So they do; and that is a reason for keeping carefully and securely our seaports, not for fixing the government at the chief port. Our European soldiers and our muskets come from England, but we do not on that account keep the Governor-General and Commander-in-Chief there. Calcutta is merely a place *en route*, and the Governor-General does not personally count muskets or weigh powder. As long as you have a fortified station to command the river and a commissary of stores at Calcutta, the seat of your government and the head-quarters of your army may be determined by other considerations than the superintendence of the transshipment of your supplies.

I say then that our maritime power is no sufficient reason for keeping our civil and military commanders in India immediately under the guns of our ships. When a child is a child he remains attached to his mother's apron-string; but when he becomes a man, if he hope to get on in the world, he goes abroad by himself, and does not remain for ever with his natural protectors, because possibly, in the event of his being sick and like to die, he may some day wish to return to them. If our Indian empire is good for anything, it is now fit to defend itself. It may be possible to have a sufficiently fortified seat of government elsewhere than at Calcutta, and in a more appropriate military situation.

In regard to climate, I need merely here say that the climate of Calcutta is tropical, and very unfavourable to European health—that at no place where it would be proposed to fix the government is there a worse climate. It remains to be seen whether we cannot find the other necessary conditions under a more favourable sky. No European remains at Calcutta longer than he can help; and the place is not, and never

Climate.

can be, a colony. It is to Europeans no more than an encampment.

The scheme of administration prevailing in Bengal was formed when our knowledge was imperfect, Government and under great disadvantages—the result and people. is not a favourable model. The Bengalese are an effeminate race, incapable of defending themselves—never found in our armies—unfit auxiliaries to a military power —and not the class whom we should most care to attach to us as our most immediate subjects—as the surrounders and supporters of our empire.

In one respect, and one respect only, is it an object to retain Calcutta as the seat of government. It would cost something to establish the Government else- Expense. where, and the question resolves itself into the degree of expense, and the comparative value of the advantages to be obtained by a transference to any other place fixed on as the best. In regard to the buildings and offices of Government, I imagine that the Government-house would be almost the only loss, and that only in so far as it is larger than (it is perhaps double) such as would have been an appropriate Government-house for Bengal alone. I believe that most of the offices of the various departments of Government are merely rented; and if the Governor of Bengal occupied one side of Government-house, and established his secretariat and some other offices in the other, the Government property would be sufficiently occupied, and it would be in the end as cheap to build offices for the departments of the Supreme Government elsewhere as to rent them in Calcutta.

Private house-property in Calcutta, of a particular description, might, no doubt, be for a time somewhat depreciated; but this, of course, cannot be considered as material in a great public question; and it is to be

I

hoped that, in so great a commercial mart, increasing prosperity and private demand would soon fill up the gap left by Government servants and offices.

I am, however, very willing to admit that, in almost any place on the continent of India which might be selected as the seat of the Supreme Government (I except Bombay, as not on the continent),

Necessity of fortifications elsewhere.

prudence would require the expenditure of more or less money in fortification, since the great native forts of former days may be little suited to modern warfare, and we have at present few fortifications of our own construction in the interior of the country. But I believe both that the best modern fortification (mud) is, in a country where manual labour is so low-priced, extremely cheap, and that money so expended would be, on general grounds, by no means thrown away. Continually advancing as we have been, it may have been prudent to abstain from sinking money in permanent works of this kind; but now that we have reached the natural limits of the empire and may hope to be more stationary, I very much doubt whether, as a foreign nation occupying a subject country, we can wisely neglect all fortification. An army in the field encamps in the open plain; but all precedents, ancient and modern, teach us that an army of permanent occupation derives great advantage from the possession of fortified *points d'appui*, in case of sudden disturbance or temporary reverse. I should say, then, that a fortified post, in the most advantageous and central position and the head-quarters of the Government and of the army, would be, on many grounds, most desirable. When we come to name particular places, we shall consider the degree of expense and the amount of collateral advantages.

I conclude, then, that Calcutta, as the seat of government, presents several most important and fatal disadvantages, and no advantage except the Conclusion in regard to Calcutta. saving of the expense involved in the change. I believe that in fact the Supreme Government of India will never be efficiently carried on at that place; that it is merely a question of time; that sooner or later a change will inevitably take place; and that the time is now come when the sooner we make up our minds to the change the better. What is the use of a nominal government at Calcutta when every Governor-General finds some reason to leave it as soon as possible, taking with him the whole power of the state? The strongest argument against fixing the government in Calcutta is, that you never will succeed in really doing so, and that it is therefore better to give it up with a good grace, and avoid all the manifold and fatal evils of a constant division of the government into two inefficient parts.

Let us see, then, what better places can be found, and whether the expense involved is so great as to induce us farther to postpone a measure so essential to the interests and good government of the empire.

Before mentioning places, we may look to the quarter of India in which it is most desirable to fix Examination of fitness of different quarters of India. the capital. The diagram (*see* title-page) shows the great provinces into which the country is now politically, and in some degree geographically, divided.

It will be seen that there are six principal divisions. A large space in the centre is occupied by a circle of the principal native states, which lie contiguous to one another in this quarter—Gwalior, Rajpootana, Hyderabad, Nagpore, &c. &c. Round this native quarter and contiguous to it (except on one side, where the desert interposes) lie the five great divisions of our territory—

Bengal, Madras, Bombay, Hindostan proper (called by us the North-West Provinces), and the plain of the Indus. In which of these great divisions should the government be fixed ?

The central quarter, being possessed almost exclusively by native states, would not be selected; and we must therefore give up the idea of finding a suitable place *quite* central to *every* part of India.

The Punjab is the frontier and outlying division, and, in some degree, isolated. The first campaign of an invading army would be there fought, and it would not be prudent nor reasonable to push so far forward our head-quarters.

Madras, though the most maritime of our territories, has not been proposed, and it is perhaps unnecessary to particularize the reasons against the selection of that province for our head-quarters.

In discussing the disadvantages of Calcutta, we have shown those of Bengal generally.

There remain, then, Bombay and Hindostan. Bombay is much the nearest to England, and the increased facilities of overland communication will soon give this fact great additional importance. With a railway across the desert, and screw-vessels in the Red Sea, the ancient line of communication may regain its former importance, and be generally used for the passage of men, stores, and valuable goods. The insular position of the town of Bombay gives it all the advantage of fortification ; it is also nearer to and within shorter communication with the frontier than Calcutta, and is conveniently situated with respect to the principal native states. It is in tolerably easy communication with our territories in Hindostan, Madras, and on the Indus ; and a railway from Bombay to Agra would be shorter, cheaper, and at least as useful, as one from Calcutta to

Agra, and would more completely unite the empire. On the other hand, the Bombay territories are the least important and prosperous, or, at any rate, the least paying, of our possessions. They are not the seats of any of our most important civil and military interests; and the experience and example of administration afforded to the members of the Supreme Government would not be satisfactory. The Governor-General would be more frequently at Bombay than he is at Calcutta, but he would have very many occasions to be absent with the army in Hindostan and on other duties. A principal objection is this—that Bombay itself is in no degree less tropical or more healthy than Calcutta; and Poonah, or some such place more healthily situated on the continent, would cost as much in fortification, &c., as other places possessing greater intrinsic advantages. On the whole, then, I should prefer Bombay to Calcutta, but think that to *it* too great and material disadvantages attach.

There remains Hindostan, the ancient seat of all the empires and dominant peoples who have ever ruled India; the most valuable possession Hindostan. in the prosperity, and the last seat of strength in the decline, of all great governments—in fact, the historical, and we may almost say natural, empress province of India, to the whole of which it has, in European parlance, even given its name. Since Hindostan has come into our possession, it has been the scene of all our most important political transactions, the basis of all great military operations. The Governor-General, in spite of the theoretical location of the government at Calcutta, has spent most of his time in these territories, and there exercised all the powers of the government; there the Commander-in-Chief, the head-quarters of the army, and the mass of our troops seem to be permanently located. *Primâ facie*, then, this province appears to be the natural and permanent seat of government. Let us see whether in detail it fulfils the required conditions.

To begin with, it lies unquestionably more central to all India than any other province in our immediate possession. It is the centre of the three great provinces (Bengal, Hindostan, and the Punjab), forming an unbroken line of the most valuable territory, now grouped together, and administered and guarded by the same service and troops. It is very conveniently situated to the principal native states, and is in easy communication with Bombay. Even from Madras, in a direct line, it is not very much farther than Calcutta. In short, we have only to look at a map to see at a glance why Akbar selected Agra as the capital of India.

Hindostan is not so near to England as Bombay, but it must be observed that it is much nearer than Bengal, and the postal communication with England is several days shorter than at Calcutta. I have already alluded to the probability of a railroad between Bombay and Agra. The Bombay line is the most advanced of Indian railroads ; it will soon run over the Ghauts, and, before long, will probably reach Malwa ; it cannot be then much longer before a central Indian rail crosses the dry and comparatively level country between Malwa and Agra, connecting the great countries of the west and centre with those of the north and east. Men and goods, despatched from London *viâ* Bombay, may then reach Agra within the month, and the old route by the Cape and Calcutta will be much less important.

Hindostan, while free from the weakness and peril of a frontier province, is as near the frontier as the capital can safely be ; and, in fact, all frontier operations, political and military, have been from hence directed. The best proof that we

Its fitness for seat of government.

could here depend on the continued presence of the Governor-General and Commander-in-Chief is in the fact that there has been hitherto no keeping them away. Here alone can we hope to retain a *united* government; and in a permanent and united government is our only chance of *good* government.

Hindostan is, and always must be, the centre of our military power. It is protected by a large outlying territory; and supposing (what is improbable) that an enemy should force the frontier passes, now watched and guarded by us, and should actually invade India, the first struggle would be in the Punjab. If we should perchance be defeated there, we may yet make a stand in Hindostan. But in Hindostan we shall fight no provincial battle; there we must rally all the forces of the empire; there we shall stake everything; there must a Governor-General and a Commander-in-Chief be present to direct a struggle of life and death; there they must concentrate their resources; and there a fortified civil and military centre will be of the utmost importance. Defeated there, we shall find no safety till we reach our ships; we must stand there, or give up India; and when we have given up India, and lost our military power, then, and not till then, we may make the most of our maritime resources, and retain the fort at Calcutta and some commercial guns to protect the commercial depôt of a commercial people trading to India. We shall have nothing more.

The climate of Hindostan is much the best in India, and it contains within its limits, places temperate, healthy, and pleasant; where we may not only advantageously locate both the European and native servants of Government, and form a capital worthy of us, but may also attain that very great desideratum as a centre and resting-place of our power—a colony.

Moreover, Hindostan forms, beyond all question and doubt, the best, and I think I may say the most important, of the subordinate governments. More matured experience, a better native system, a finer people, a more uniform language, some gifted individuals bestowed by fortune, the more immediate presence and interest of the heads of the government, and, it may be added, the superior energy and efficiency in Europeans and natives due to the superior climate, have all combined to make this province the model and success of our system. Here alone could the members of the Supreme Government learn a system worthy of generalisation. Upon the people of Hindostan we chiefly rely for our service and support, and them especially must it be our object particularly to attach to us. Most of the opium is produced in Hindostan * which is merely sold in Calcutta as an entrepôt, and there credited, and, setting aside this item, we shall find that in the chief local sources of revenue (especially land revenue), it is superior, and, even including the sea customs and other imperial incomes levied at Calcutta, is little inferior in total revenue to Bengal. Altogether, and in every way, we have a greater interest in the internal administration of Hindostan than of any other province.

I have then, I think, gone through the various conditions, and upon any general ground whatever I confess that I can scarcely conceive a doubt as to the propriety of fixing the central government of India in Hindostan.

We have yet to consider the particular place in that province which presents the greatest advantages. Delhi and Agra boast an ancient, and Simla a sort of modern prescription. As between Delhi and Agra there can be no doubt that

Question of particular locality in Hindostan.

* One opium-producing division, "Bahar," though a province of Hindostan, belongs to the Bengal government.

Agra is much preferable, and we may therefore dismiss Delhi from the question.

With respect to Agra, I think it may be asserted that it is not now to so great an extent a native, social, or political capital as to give it any very great claim on that ground alone. Agra has been only within the last few years made the seat of the government of the N.W. provinces, and it has not been found by any means necessary that the Lieutenant-Governor should continually reside there. The local business has no particular importance. The city is one of several of the most important towns within the limits of the government; but as I have before said, neither this nor any other place is at the present day intrinsically the native capital either of India or of Hindostan. The fact, then, is, that as concerns the natives we are free to select for our capital whatever place may best suit us, provided only that it be conveniently situated for their access, settlement, and residence. If in these respects there is no obstacle, they will soon flock in sufficient numbers round the permanent seat of our government and government establishments, and probably before long form a native city, as important as any which now exists, and which will in course of time become much more so. It is wonderful how soon on the site of the bazaars of a mere military encampment a city springs up.

This being the case, we may fairly, without detriment to the natives, consider also the interests of the Europeans, and of the European government, as involved in those of its servants and European subjects.

To them the possession of a temperate climate is of the very utmost consequence. I fear that, in the investigations of Parliament, due consideration has not been given to the vast importance of climate, not for the mere personal

Importance of climate in the consideration

comfort of individuals, but as in fact and actual practice and experience most important, I may say essential,
to the organization, working, and success of a govern-
—of a seat of ment which must consist of Europeans,
government;   and in which an unfavourable climate
causes a succession of absences, divisions, and changes
altogether fatal to good government,. destroys bodily and
mental energy, and renders necessary much enhanced
remuneration for much inferior service. This disadvantage may be inevitable to some countries, but, if in India
we can choose between a good and a bad climate, why
should we prefer the bad? In that country prudent
men send their very dogs of European birth and breed-
ing to the hills in the hot weather. Are not then our
governors and councillors more precious than grey-
hounds? But there has been too great apprehension of
the imputation of personal motives. Most of those
who have given their evidence to the committees of
Parliament have been, or hope to be, members of the
government; and although nearly all have in practice
been driven by public duty to the hills, none will bring
prominently forward mere personal health and vigour as
the valid arguments in determining the seat of government which they really are. It is not any private consideration which should weigh, but the health and efficiency of the government individually and collectively.
The sanitary condition of his most valuable servants
is of very considerable importance to the master.

And it is not only to the immediate members of the
—of a European government that the climate of the capital
social capital;   is of such consequence. The general body
of the European servants of government, and those
connected with them, form a vast and most important
class. To them the permanent head-quarters of government and of the army, if favourably situated and

in a good climate, will form, and it is highly desirable that they should form, a social capital of India (which Calcutta is not), where they will congregate for business, health, and pleasure, where they will become known to the heads of the government and to one another, and where there may be some interchange of ideas. The hard-worked government servant, who has a short leave from his solitary home in the jungles, will there not only fallow his mind by idleness, but will improve it by communications and acquire civilised associations. Especial advantage will be derived from the existence of a common ground on which official and professional men from all different parts of India will meet and learn to share with one another their varied mass of information; and not less will be the gain from the meeting and intercommunication of English and Indian servants, of head-quarter men and provincials, and of official men in general, with the non-official European residents in the country, who will doubtless frequent a European capital. All these advantages are lost if the capital be fixed in a bad and tropical climate, which has no attraction to non-residents, and is avoided by all as much as possible.

I have also alluded to the possibility of combining a colony with a capital. This is not the place to discuss the whole question of the —of a colony. mode and degree in which we may with advantage attempt to colonise in India, and to amalgamate with the natives; but it may be generally asserted (with reference to the true and often repeated fact that we are yet but encamped in the country) that it would be a great additional strength, and afford many incidental advantages, if we could make our capital something of the nature of a colony—a centre of a resident European and mixed population—a home and an asylum for

natives who may have adopted or approached our
manners, our society, or our religion, or have inter-
mixed with our blood—a nucleus of European education,
arts, and manufactures—and a rest whereon to place the
lever with which we may gradually move the whole
mass of India.

Experience has proved that in ordinary private business unaided Europeans cannot compete with natives,
and that no private colonization takes place. But the
fixed centre of a European government, the service
of that government, the supply of its demands and
of those of a European capital and large European
residence, would at once furnish the necessary attraction
for European and mixed labour ; and if we can find a
place combining some natural capabilities with a temperate climate, the classes referred to will undoubtedly
colonise. It is, as has been said, essential that the
place should not be unfitted for natives ; but if we can
combine the two conditions, a very great object will be
attained. All things then considered, we may compare
the different places which present themselves.

Agra is admirably well situated for the seat of
government in many respects. But though
the climate is much better than Calcutta,
it is yet very hot indeed in the summer. It is a tropical
climate, and the difference between it and that of Calcutta is not radical, but only one of degree. It is on this
account quite unsuited for a European capital. Moreover, the fort of Agra, though large, and in good preser-
vation, is probably not a good place of modern defence ;
and, situated as Agra is, it might be necessary to expend
a very considerable sum in fortification, in order to render
both the offices and treasury of government and the native
city fully defensible against any *coup de main*.

Simla, again, is in a fine climate, and a very pretty

Objections to Agra ;

and pleasant place, but is in other respects very inconveniently situated. It is too far to the north, and is so far in the interior of the and to Simla. hills as to be very difficult of access. It is deficient in labour and supplies; altogether unsuited for a native, and most inconvenient for a European capital; and with no capabilities for a colony. I think that the objections to making Simla the permanent seat of government are insurmountable.

But there is another place not yet brought into importance by the residence of members of the Government, but already as a place Proposed site at Mussoorie-Dey-rah. of private residence more frequented, and infinitely more accessible, cheap, and convenient than Simla. Mussoorie is not so well clothed and pretty as Simla, but it is in as agreeable and cool a climate, and decidedly more healthy. And it possesses the great advantage indispensable to a permanent capital, that it immediately overlooks the plains of Hindostan; and within five miles as the road now winds down the hill, or a much shorter distance in a straight line, is a very large fertile valley, exceedingly well suited both for native residence and resort and for European colonization, and abounding in labour and supplies. The hills of Mussoorie afford space enough for any number of European houses, a portion of which might be built close together in European style, while detached residences would extend beyond the limits of the present station. Such a post could be impregnably fortified at a very small expense of money, and defended by a very small number of men. But one of the greatest advantages remains to be told. The valley or plain immediately under the hill-station—the spot in which would be the native capital, and which is already much desiderated and partially colonized by European and native

Christian settlers—is walled in, as it were, from the great plain of Hindostan by the lower or Sewalic chain of hills —a sort of segment of a circle which surrounds the valley, and on either side closes into the great mountain range. This wall is low and comparatively narrow, but one mass of ravines and gullies, and in a natural state impracticable. Roads can be made through it, such that it becomes no obstacle whatever to the easiest communication ; and yet, except by these defensible passes or gates, it cannot be entered. It is the best of natural fortifications.

In short, the spot to which I allude, immediately overlooking the whole plain of Hindostan at the point where its great rivers issue from the hills, and in every way conveniently situated, seems as if it had been expressly formed by nature to fulfil the almost incompatible conditions required by us for a perfectly convenient seat of the European government of an Indian empire. The valley is the Deyrah Dhoon, and the position of the places referred to will be seen from the accompanying sketch.

Mussoorie, instead of being remote and isolated like Simla, is perched on the outer range of hills immediately north of Agra and Delhi, with which places it communicates by the best road in India through our most fertile and flourishing territory. It is at a point where the outer Himmalayas rise unusually high ; on an impregnable clump of hills rising abruptly from the plain, and flanked on either side by the Ganges and Jumna, which, here rushing deep and impetuous from the mountains, and cutting narrow chasms in the Sewalic range, may be seen from Mussoorie winding their way far into the plains. Immediately below is the head of the great Ganges Canal, along the bank of which a railway may be run from Allahabad to Deyrah for the mere cost

Its situation and advantages.

PROPOSED SITE OF THE CAPITAL OF INDIA.

MUSSOOREE

DEYRAH

Protecting Batteries

Road

Railway to Bombay and Calcutta

Detached Fort

Fort

Fort

Detached Fort

Tea Plantations

Small Stream

Small Stream

Small Stream

S E W A L I C R A N G E

GANGES

JUMNA

Lith. by J. Netemann, 9, Charing Cross.

Published by John Murray, Albemarle Street, London 1853.

of the iron rails, and without involving an additional brick or spade of earth. The present station of Mussoorie is on an average about 7000 feet above the sea; contains a very large number of detached houses; and there is still a considerable range of unoccupied hill rising even higher. The climate is altogether temperate, and unquestionably the best and most healthy yet discovered in India. It is well supplied with water, and everything is as cheap and plentiful as in the most favoured spots of the plain country.

Deyrah is a particularly beautiful place, in a country which is quite a garden abounding in water and vegetation such as natives delight in, and a favourite resort of Europeans except when the heats of summer drive them for a time to the overhanging heights. The passes through the Sewalic range are even now practicable to all kinds of wheeled carriages, and at a very little expense the road might be made one of the best in the country. Immediately beyond the Sewalic range lies a broad and populous territory, abounding in productions of every kind, and watered by those two riches-bestowing rivers not inaptly deified by the Hindoos. Between them is the great Doab, the pride of Hindostan, and it is flanked by the fertile and famous provinces of Rohilcund and Sirhind.

Mussoorie-Deyrah, in fact, combines almost all the advantages of Agra and Simla, with several others besides. It is within such easy reach of the former place that it is little inferior in the advantage of a central position and speedy communication with all parts of India and with England, and it is admirably placed for the superintendence of frontier politics and military matters. Mussoorie is a better residence and capital for Europeans than Simla, and Deyrah for natives than Agra.

To make Mussoorie altogether impregnable would cost,

I imagine, next to nothing; and it is difficult to conceive
a place better suited for the head-quarters
Fortifications of.
of an army acting on the defensive, or for
the refuge, trysting, and recruiting place of a beaten
or inferior force, than the Deyrah Dhoon, that pleasant
valley flowing with water, abounding in corn and oil,
defended by two most difficult rivers and the most perfect natural fortification which can be imagined, and surmounted by an impregnable citadel. If still further security be desired, the nature of the country would make
it very easy, by the aid of the natural ravines and other
assistance, to form on the side of the valley sloping down
from the foot of the Mussoorie precipices a semicircular
line of fortifications somewhat as shown in the annexed
diagram, which should make the native capital defensible
in case our outer defences were forced, and would enable
us to retain to the utmost extremity our last hold of
Hindostan. I do not anticipate that matters will soon
come to this point, but it is merely conceding to those
who argue the necessity of a very secure capital that I
point out the treble security of the proposed site.

The expense of a Government-house would not be a
great consideration in so important a matter; it would
be as cheap to build offices at Mussoorie and Deyrah as
to rent them in Calcutta; and the servants of government would build for themselves.

Here then at last we might have a stable and energetic government. Neither health nor constantly recur-
ring political and military business would carry away
the Governor-General, the Commander-in-Chief, or the
other members of the government. They would never
be absent except on short cold-weather tours, or on very
extraordinary occasions. Here we might concentrate
the whole of our European energies; here we should
retain the services of men of whom we are now deprived

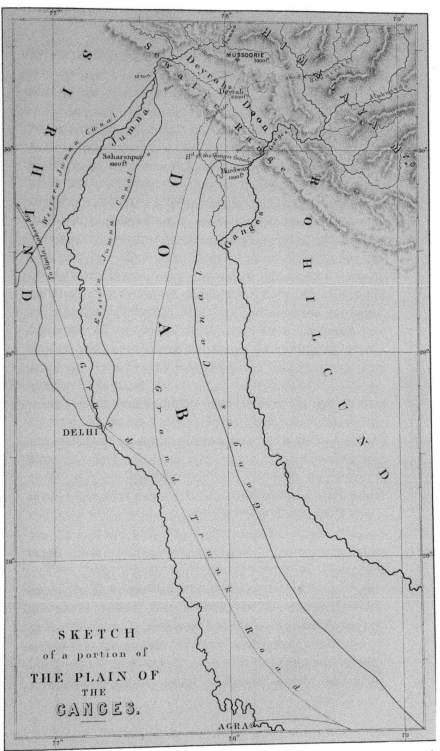

SKETCH
of a portion of
THE PLAIN OF
THE
GANGES.

Published by John Murray, Albemarle Street, London 1853.

by the climate; and here we might found an imperial
system worthy of the reputation of the rulers and the
greatness of the country ruled.

I would propose, then, permanently to fix at Mussoorie-Deyrah both the Supreme Government and that of Hindostan, and the head-quarters of the army, with all their offices and establishments. I would have at Mussoorie a European Government-house, the English offices, and the residence of the European officers; at the foot of the hill a native durbar-hall, the public sittings of the chief courts of justice, the principal educational establishments for the natives, the head-quarters of the ordnance and commissariat, the body-guard and personal escort, and other native establishments. The Governor-General and other European officers might come down for a few hours any day that native business was to be done, and in the cold weather would probably spend some time in the valley among the natives. *Proposed arrangements,*

Around Deyrah might probably be formed a cantonment of native troops drawn from the neighbouring stations to form a head-quarter force; and the European regiments and artillerymen would be perched on the surrounding hills in the hot season, and descend to the valley for exercise in the cold weather. By a new road and fixed steam-engines the communication between the hill and the valley might be reduced to the smallest expenditure of labour and time.

The valley would become a colony of European, mixed, and native settlers and followers of our power. And those natives who for us *and results.* or for the truth's sake sacrifice their own social position would find themselves no longer outcasts.

There tea, and sugar, and hops, and oats, and many European products would be largely grown, and there

K

we should have schools of art, and model cotton-mills and iron-foundries, and many other things besides.

In short, the settlement would be in every way the suitable centre and nucleus of our peculiarly situated power—would supply many deficiencies and secure many hitherto unattainable advantages—the government would be carried on as it ought to be—the Indian service of England would be no longer a penance and a pain— and we should have a connecting link between natives and Europeans. A more pleasant, beautiful, and interesting spot would not exist. The Indian capital would become a fashionable winter resort. Instead of going to Brighton, people would take out through-tickets in November from London Bridge to Deyrah, and spend an Indian "season" at an Indian capital. The great Asiatic possession of England would acquire the interest and importance which is its due, and from one point, thoroughly our own, our religion, science, and civilization might at last be in reality diffused throughout India.

In so great an imperial undertaking we should not be niggard of reasonable expense. The country well *Necessary expenditure.* managed can afford the funds for so necessary an expenditure. Yet, in the first instance, I would not propose anything at all proportionate to what is expended in this or any other country on the seats of the national Government: witness, for instance, our new Houses of Parliament.

Say that 1,000,000*l.* sterling were allowed to found an Indian capital; 500,000*l.* for public buildings, &c., and 500,000*l.* for fortifications and outworks, would be, I should think, in the first instance, amply sufficient. In future, all money expended for useful purposes would go infinitely farther than much larger sums unsystematically disbursed for similar objects in different places throughout India.

I have dwelt so long on this subject because, hoping, as I do, that our empire in India will be lasting, it is of the greatest importance that we should possess a suitable capital and colony, and the question should now be permanently settled. It is a great pity in any way to postpone it. At the same time we must not decide a matter of this kind on any mere temporary considerations. We must have a capital which may be still a capital a hundred years hence. For instance, no one can doubt that the great lines of railway will eventually be completed. It is only a question of a few years sooner or later; and I think that in discussing the merits of Bombay and Agra or Mussoorie I am fully justified in assuming that there will be a railroad between those places, and that the traffic between Northern India and England will take the most direct route to the western coast. The trunk railway through the plain of the Ganges will be abundantly useful to 'that populous country; but it is quite certain that as soon as we have a system of railways, and goods and passengers are carried by rail instead of by river, Bombay will be almost exclusively the port of Northern and Central India, and Calcutta only that of Bengal, Bahar, and perhaps Benares. We have but to look to the map to be sure of this fact, the more so as Bombay is an infinitely more convenient and cheaper harbour than Calcutta. The latter is situated a long way up a most uncertain river, which involves much risk and expense, and a freak of the Ganges may any day make it an inland town. Indeed, the tendency of the river is quite in that direction, for, where British fleets once manœuvred, the navigation is now confined to flat river-boats. We may, therefore, reckon without our host if we fix on Calcutta as a continuing city.

No one doubts the evils which have resulted from the

K 2

division of the government. But some people say, "Oh,
Alternative if it is very true that the Governor-General is
plan rejected. often obliged to leave Calcutta, but that
would do no harm if he only took his counsellors with
him." This I believe to be altogether a mistake. It
is not only for want of advice that the government
absent from head-quarters is inefficient for great and
deliberate undertakings, but also on account of its separation from its offices, records, and establishments—from its
accustomed ways, and habits, and channels of reference
—from its roots and branches, as it were. The Governor-General may at a considerable expense carry about
with him his counsellors, but it is quite impossible that
he should carry about with him all the vast establishments and machines subordinate to him. For local and
personal duties temporary tours through the country are
most useful, and not inconsistent with the conduct of the
ordinary and most necessary current affairs of the empire ; but for general review and superintendence, for the
undertaking and digestion of great measures, I maintain
that a permanent head-quarters and a united government
are absolutely indispensable. The Governor-General at
Simla and the Council at Calcutta are each quite inefficient for such purposes. Every executive officer in charge
of a district feels the same thing. He goes into camp in
the cold weather, and marches through his district, but
all his most serious and important business is done when
he is at his head-quarters with his full office establishment, and following a regular course of life and business.
It is just the same with the government. You may as
well expect a tree transplanted every six months to bear
fruit, as a government which has no permanent abiding-
place. In no executive office in India can you or
ought you to depend on permanent residence in the cold
weather. That is the season for movement, and at that

time business tours should be not only permitted, but
encouraged and ordered. It is, therefore, in the summer
that the most regular and deliberate business is done.
It is also in the summer that there is temptation to seek
a good climate ; and if you fix your seat of government
in a bad climate, and permit the members of the government to be habitually absent in the hot season for the
sake of health, or on other grounds, all hope of efficiency
is gone. .You must, therefore, either determine for
reasons already urged to fix the government in a good
climate, or you must positively prohibit the Governor-
General from going to the hills without permission—must
subject him and the other members of the government
to exactly the same rules and restrictions as other European servants ; and when health fails, you must appoint
a new man, just as you would to any other office. I say
that there is no medium between these two principles of
action at all consistent with efficiency, and that you
must adopt one or the other.

If Calcutta is to be the seat of government, let us
choose the less of two evils. It is better that our
governors should be hot and frequently changed than
that the whole government should be inefficient. Calcutta, therefore, let it be, in earnest and not in name.
Absolutely restrict business tours to the cold weather
months — intrust the politics of the frontier without
reserve to the local governor—bring down to Calcutta
the Commander-in-Chief and head-quarter staff—and let
all future absences be confined by precise leave-rules. I
shall propose those rules in connection with the civil
service, and need here only say that I would restrict
temporary or local leave to six months in three years,
taken either in portions or at once, and without transferring the responsibilities of office ; and that after
seven years' resident service I would allow one year's

general leave, the duties being intrusted to a deputy, subject to instructions, and two-thirds of the salary being cut.

We have yet to consider the great executive divisions Local govern- into which, under the Supreme Govern-ments. ment, India must be portioned out. I think that the six principal provinces enumerated at page 116 will be the most natural divisions, and most nearly coinciding with previous arrangements.

It might be possible to unite the Punjab *cis* the The plain of the Indus with the government of the North-Indus a fifth West Provinces, making over Benares to government. Bengal, leaving Scinde with Bombay, and putting the strip of territory and political duties beyond the Indus under a separate frontier political agent. But, first, it is by no means an object to unite inconveni-ently large territories under one executive government, since personal gubernatorial supervision has been much wanting in India ; and second, it would be highly incon-venient to divide between three separate authorities the plain of the Indus, the whole of which is the outwork of India, and has so recently fallen into our possession. Politically and socially there is much that is common to the whole line of the Indus, and to the whole of that large territory, between Sirhind and the trans-Indus hills, which has been, till recently, more constantly and exclusively a Mahommedan possession, and latterly the seat of that independent Sikh monarchy which rolled back the Mahommedan power on the one hand, and threatened Hindostan on the other. Both as being con-tiguous and intimately connected countries, and in order to promote the Indus route of communication, navigation, and commerce, I think it especially desirable to unite Scinde with the Punjab, instead of drawing across a particular point on the river a division line between two governments and armies far distant from and communicating but little with one another.

I would therefore make the plain of the Indus a separate and fifth subordinate government, a character to which its position and importance give it every claim.

The sixth great division is the aggregation of native states in Central India. It would be highly inconvenient that these should be parcelled out to the separate management of separate governments; still more so that each should be left to the varied views, character, and colouring of individual political agents. In no department is there so great an absence of any general, fixed, or recorded rules of conduct, and in none are individual servants of the government so liable to be blinded or prejudiced as the residents at native courts, isolated as they are in an atmosphere of native intrigue. They are apt to take up strongly particular views, and, having once adopted them, are often urged by the inimitable native talent for colouring, exaggerating, and telling one-sided stories, into honest but violent partisanship.* The Supreme Government cannot possibly look with sufficient closeness into all the details of every native state great and small, and therefore I think it would be well to profit by the fact of the great mass of these states lying contiguous in the centre of the country, and to adopt Sir John Malcolm's plan of a Chief Political Commissioner for Central India, immediately under the Supreme Government, who, free from the exclusive bias of particular Residents, might superintend all these central states,† and introduce some uniformity and system in their management.

Chief Political Commissioner of Central India.

* Outram Blue Book again.
† Including Hyderabad, Nagpore, Gwalior, Baroda, Rajpootana, &c.

The local chieftains isolated in the midst of our territories might be included in the local governments, while
the Residents at Nepal and Oude (till the latter country
is administered by us) would report direct to the
Supreme Government.

Of our own territories there would then be five local
governments—

Bengal,

Madras,

Bombay,

Hindostan—(the term N.W. Provinces having become
inappropriate)—and

The Indus territories.

First, of the personal constitution of these governments.

An important question arises on the threshold.   Shall

Position of the Governor-General in a local government. the Governor-General be a member of the
local government of the province where
the Supreme Government is located, and,
if so, in what position?   It is admitted on all hands that
the greatest inconvenience has resulted from the present
practice of making the Governor-General Governor of
Bengal, with the mere power of delegating his duties
temporarily from time to time to a member of council,
in practice the senior for the time being.   It is
unnecessary to dwell on the manifold practical evils
which have resulted from this system.   But two arguments are urged on the other side—that the local
government is the only opportunity afforded to the
Governor-General of acquiring knowledge and practice
of inferior details, and that the patronage attached
thereto is necessary to his consequence and dignity.

The first of these arguments may be a very good
reason for not appointing a Governor-General destitute
of experience of Indian affairs, but can be none for

loading him with duties which he cannot by possibility properly perform. If it is necessary that he should have experience of inferior duties, it must be acquired before and not after his appointment as Governor-General: A man cannot perform at the same time two incompatible tasks. We may hope that, under such a system as I have proposed, we should have a class of superior statesmen not altogether destitute of Indian experience; but if a new man must be put in as Governor-General, the only remedy is to let him remain long enough to acquire, and make use of, the experience of his own office. I would give him every facility for seeing and understanding the subordinate duties, but would not sacrifice the interest and welfare of our greatest provinces in order that, by now and then dividing with local duties the time which is fully required for the Supreme Government, he may gain some experience of the one to the neglect of the other.

The practical, working, local government must (if the management of all India is to be intrusted to a Governor-General) be the duty of a separate and permanent Governor; but both for the education of the Governor-General, and because the local governor on the spot can be more minutely supervised than other governors, I would make him an officer of somewhat inferior rank, and in more direct subordination to the Governor-General,—would put him, in fact, on much the same footing as the present Lieutenant-Governor of the N.W. Provinces. There would be no objection to make the Governor-General the nominal Governor—to give to him individually a full control over the proceedings of his Lieutenant (as he now has), and the right to know, advise regarding, and in some measure, when he so pleases, direct, all that is going on, besides exercising such share of the patronage as he sees fit. But the Lieutenant must still be a permanent, responsible, Governor. The Governor-General will be merely individually his counsellor and officially his superior, but will not necessarily relieve him of any part of his duties, and will only interfere exceptionally when he thinks it expedient so to do. The reasons for relieving the Governor-General of the local details of a subordinate government apply equally to the Non-Regulation Provinces, which must all be included in the local governments; and it is on this account that some definite arrangement regarding the Punjab is absolutely necessary.

I think that the patronage of the appointments connected with the Supreme Government, the discretionary power over the patronage of the local lieutenant-governor, and the reservation of some control over the higher appointments in all the subordinate governments under a special and separate rule, would amply provide the Governor-General with patronage. Too much small patronage is the very opposite of an advantage.

For the other four provinces I would have governors, Governors. as there now are at Madras and Bombay, but over whom a more immediate direction and control would be exercised than has hitherto been the case.

The objection to idle counsellors in the Supreme Government applies with much greater Counsellors hitherto existing. force to Madras and Bombay. At these presidencies one counsellor is nominally chief of the principal court of justice in each; and at Madras the other holds the same position in the Board of Revenue. It may have been intended as an extremely rational arrangement merely, without additional expense, to enable and require the Governor to call into council the heads of departments; but if, as I understand it, the counsellors are in fact additional appointments, mere nominal, or at any rate supernumerary members of the courts and board, and to whom, on the other hand, the Governor has no power of delegating any portion of his actual duties, in this character they seem to be unnecessary, if not worse. One objection which has been urged to a change is, that, there being at Madras and Bombay separate armies, and consequent military business, counsellors are thereby rendered necessary. But I confess that I am quite unable to see how the addition to the government of two civil members of council can make it in any way more competent to deal with military matters. I would make the Commanders-in-Chief at Madras and Bombay (if the armies remain separate) *ex-officio* members of council in military matters; and they would find it at least as easy to deal with one civilian as with three. The army of Bengal would remain as at present, under the Supreme Government. Another argument is, that, as the Supreme Government appointments have hitherto been for the most part given to Bengal servants, it would be unfair to those of Madras and Bombay not to leave council appointments in their own presidencies, to reward their services. This I answer, first, by again saying that public appointments must be made with reference not to past but to present work; and second, by referring to my former proposal, that all the appointments of the Supreme Government should be given to the most eligible men from all the presidencies without distinction.

In fact, it seems to me to be clear that an efficient local governor, being not so much a deliberative as an executive officer, would be much more effective wielding single and active power in his own person than with a council; and it must be particularly observed that he has in fact in each presidency regularly constituted boards and heads of departments, civil and military, his responsible and legitimate advisers, and is in this respect much more favourably situated than the Governor-General. Still, this much may be admitted, that if, as at present, English governors, totally unacquainted with India, are sometimes sent to the subordinate presidencies, there would be inconvenience in the want of any immediate responsible adviser. And I should also say, that where there are large commercial cities and European communities (as Calcutta, Bombay, and Madras), an unaided governor cannot well perform all his local duties, and at the same time have it in his power to make tours in the interior, and exercise the necessary personal supervision. On general grounds it would be in future highly desirable to abstain from the appointment of inexperienced men as local executive governors. But it is so great an object to keep open a school for future Governors-General, that I would not exclude by rule unprofessional persons. I would, however, propose a plan to obviate the difficulties which I have noticed, by the following scheme.

Instead of councils, each of the governors of Bengal, Madras, and Bombay, to have a deputy-governor, to whom he shall be authorised to delegate, from time to time, any portion of his duties, and who shall be also his counsellor and responsible adviser, on the same footing as the present counsellors. In every presidency at least one member of the government shall be a servant of ten years' service in India, appointed by the Governor-General.

Proposed deputy-governors.

The plan of a deputy or joint-governor is exactly that which works well in other executive departments. A magistrate and collector in charge of a district has a joint-magistrate, capable of exercising any portion of his own powers, but subordinate to him. The deputy-governor, instead of being a mere idle adviser, will take a share of the work, particular business or departments for which he is most fitted being intrusted to him by the governor; and he will either take charge of the head-quarter office and local business while the governor is absent, or may be sent on tours of inspection while the governor remains stationary. The Governor of the Indus territory, and the Lieutenant-Governor of Hindostan, having comparatively little local business, will not need assistance till Mussoorie-Deyrah becomes a great city, and then, when the Lieutenant-Governor is absent on tours of inspection, and the Governor-General has not time to spare, the minister of the interior might take temporary local charge.

The rule in regard to the persons to be nominated will leave it optional to appoint to places in the government a limited number of Appointment to these posts. persons without professional qualifications; but unless the deputy-governor be professionally qualified, an unprofessional person cannot be appointed governor, and *vice versâ*. The Lieutenant-Governor of Agra, and Governor of the Indus territory, being alone, must be professional men.

I would give to the Senate power to appoint from England to every vacancy for which a non-professional man is eligible persons in or out of the service; and to all other vacancies (or, failing an appointment by the Senate) the Governor-General would nominate from the service in India, a veto being reserved to the Senate. All these appointments would be for five years, and the holders re-eligible; on the same footing as the superior officers of the Supreme Government.

The secretaries to the local governments will not be in the same position as the ministers of the Supreme

Government, because the boards and other heads of departments fill the corresponding situations; and the secretary is (or ought to be if the governor is efficient) merely the ministerial organ of communication. A secretary in each presidency, with two deputies in Bengal and Madras, and one in Hindostan, Bombay, and the Indus territory, will be amply sufficient.

The local governments, then, will stand thus, with the annual salaries affixed:—

		£.	£.
Bengal—			
Governor	. . . . .	12,000	
Deputy	. . . . .	7,000	
Secretaries	. . . .	6,000	
			25,000
Madras—			
Governor, deputy, and secretaries, as above	.	25,000	
Commander-in-Chief, in addition to military pay		2,000	
			27,000
Bombay—			
Governor	. . . .	10,000	
Deputy	. . . .	6,000	
Commander-in-Chief	. . . . .	2,000	
Secretaries	. . . . . .	5,000	
			23,000
Hindostan—			
Governor-General *ex officio* Governor.			
Lieutenant-Governor	. . . . .	10,000	
Secretaries	. . . . . .	4,000	
			14,000
Indus Territory—			
Governor	. . . . . .	12,000	
Secretaries	. . · . . .	4,000	
			16,000
Grand Total	. . . .	**£105,000**	

Expense. (margin note beside Bengal)

The position of the local governments, in subordination to the Supreme Government, has been generally noticed in explaining the proposed powers and duties of the latter. The provincial governments would be in every respect subject to its orders, and would transmit information of their proceedings in

Powers, &c. (margin note)

such form as may be directed. But I have suggested that, under a constitutional code, the Supreme Government should delegate to its subordinates certain powers of local legislation, &c.

The plan of submitting for approval at the commencement of each year a sort of provincial budget, embodying the proposed financial arrangements, seems a very good one. It might be left to the subordinate governments to arrange details within the limits of the budget, and subject to such interference as might be deemed necessary. For all excess beyond a limited margin special sanction would be necessary. The idea of permitting any government to spend money at its discretion, while it is under no sort of obligation to find funds to meet the expenditure, is altogether absurd.

In the disposal of patronage, it might be a good plan to require the concurrence of the Supreme Government in the highest class of appointments, and to leave the rest to the local governors, as is now the case in the north-west provinces.

I would have the local governors absolute in their own duties, subject only to the obligation of taking advice where there are advisers. The deputy-governors, in all things, and the Commander-in-Chief in all military matters, should be made cognizant of all proceedings, and should record their opinions, after which, the governor may act on his own responsibility, in case of difference immediately reporting the proceedings to the Supreme Government.

The places at which the subordinate governments shall be fixed must depend so much on local cir- Location.
cumstances that I shall not pretend a precise opinion in regard to all of them; but I would still bear in mind the public advantage of a good climate; would, as far as possible, consult the health and comfort

of the officers of government; and would keep in view the principles referred to in discussing the seat of the Supreme Government.

There is no doubt that Calcutta must remain the seat of the government of Bengal. I have already proposed Mussoorie-Deyrah for that of Hindostan. Lahore, having ceased to be the capital of the Sikh monarchy, and not being the old capital of the Sikh nation and religion, is not necessarily a seat of government. The Indus government might perhaps be advantageously and securely fixed on the outer range of hills overlooking the central Punjab—say near the issue of the Jhelum, which is also the most navigable of the Punjab rivers.

I do not know whether it would be possible to remove the Madras government to Bangalore; but if not, the governor or deputy might now and then be permitted to spend the hot weather on the hills in the western portion of the presidency, and at the same time recruit his vigour and overlook the business of the districts in that direction.

The Bombay government seems to have established a migratory system. Perhaps the government and chief courts, &c., might be fixed at Poonah, which is in easy communication with Bombay, and shortly will be more so. But the insular position and commercial importance of Bombay itself render the expediency of such a step doubtful. It will never do, however, that the governor, spending the hot weather and rains at Mahableshwar and Poonah, should have only the cold weather to visit his head-quarters, and no time whatever to make *bonâ fide* tours in his provinces. He must either fix his permanent residence at Bombay or move it elsewhere.

The chief political commissioner of Central India might have his head-quarters in the Saugor territory, which is our own. Hoshungabad, on the Nerbudda, would be perhaps a good place.

It only remains to provide for the contingency of its being deemed inexpedient to render the Supreme Government, by a change of constitution, duties, and place, equal to the efficient superintendence of all India. In that case, I see nothing for it but to transfer the central power to England (great as would be the disadvantages of such a step), and to put the minor governments ordinarily under the direction, not of the Governor-General, but of the Senate at home. One governor of superior dignity should, in this case, have a power of control in emergencies; and it is desirable that the political power of dealing with native states should be concentrated in one hand. But for this purpose it would not be necessary to have a separate Supreme Government. For the same reasons urged in fixing the site of the Supreme Government, I would give this controlling power to the Governor or Governor-General of Hindostan, and would include in that province the Indus territory and Central India. Under the Governor-General of Hindostan I would have a deputy-governor of Hindostan Proper, on the same footing as the deputy-governors of other presidencies, and, when not charged with separate duties, he should act as minister of the interior, both for Hindostan and for emergent interferences in other governments. The Indus territory I would intrust to a lieutenant-governor, subject to the Governor-General, on exactly the same footing as the present lieutenant-governor N. W. Provinces. The chief political commissioner of Central India would be like a lieutenant-governor under the Governor-General, who should also have a responsible political minister. The Commander-in-Chief would be, *ex officio*, counsellor in military

Arrangements, if have no central government.

L

matters, and the deputy-governor, political minister, and Commander-in-Chief would form, collectively, a consultative council.

In case of the absence of the Governor-General on political duties, the deputy-governor, fully conversant with all details, would at once become the efficient Governor of Hindostan, under the control of the Governor-General.

Bengal, Bombay, and Madras, would take their ordinary instructions from the Senate direct, and would refer to the Senate their legislation and finance.

I have referred to those natural boundaries of India External rela- which we have already reached, and to tions. which I would adhere. Happily the country is so well fenced in by nature that our external relations may be confined within a narrow space.

We possess a compact, peaceable, and nearly isolated empire; and while so great a field lies before us within that empire, it will indeed be a misfortune if, deserting our natural limits, we plunge into the centre of another continent, and enter on another warlike and expensive career, to promote an inconsiderable commerce, to impose upon barbarians the diplomacy of civilized nations, or to gratify our warlike propensities.

The possession of Burmah is, as regards India, quite The eastern unnecessary, and the advantage of acquir- frontier. ing that country must be altogether judged per se. I have no sufficient information to enable me to form a decided opinion in regard to such a step; but before committing ourselves we should well ascertain several things :—First, who the people of Burmah in fact are—whether they are a race patient of political subjection, or impatient of a foreign yoke? If the latter, the country will never pay. Second, whether the revenue is large enough to support our expensive government and expensive military establishment without aid from India?

Third, who will be our neighbours—what is the country to the east of Burmah—shall we be free from troublesome hill tribes, and from the necessity of farther advance? Unless these questions are satisfactorily answered, the prudence of advancing our frontier may well be doubted. India having already a sufficient eastern boundary, being in no way threatened in that quarter, and even in so great security that it has been found unnecessary to keep any considerable number of troops in the east of Bengal, there can be no reason whatever that it should pay for keeping Burmah, if Burmah does not pay the whole of its own charges, direct and indirect. The great facilities for navigation afforded by the Irawaddy render the country so accessible that we have (it is to be hoped), under any circumstances, little reason to fear another Affghan disaster—but then it must be remembered that no one dreamt of occupying Affghanistan for its own sake. We sought but to make it a barrier against more distant and more powerful nations. Burmah subserves no such purpose ; and therefore, even if we can hold it more cheaply and securely than Affghanistan, we have not the same grounds for doing so, and ought not to go to *any* expense with that view. Even if the Burmese cannot pay the expenses of the war, we need not farther punish ourselves for their barbarity. We need not throw good money after bad. If Burmah will not pay, let us beat the Burmese, vindicate our honour, obtain for the British merchant the 90*l.* of which the imperfect administration of justice in the Burmese territories has deprived him, and sail away home again.

It is not even necessary to have any diplomatic relations with the Burmese. Trade, after all, had better be left to the natural effect of mutual interests, and it is even better not to trade with the Burmese than to force our goods on them at the point of the bayonet. As to the Americans, I am not aware that they have ever threatened to occupy Burmah, and, if they do, we must treat or fight with the Americans, not with the Burmese. We may object to the occupation of Burmah by the Americans, just as the Americans would object to the occupation of Mexico by us.

To adopt the half-measure of annexing the lower part of the valley of the Irawaddy and leaving the upper part, seems to me to be the worst policy of all; for we thus voluntarily abandon a natural boundary to establish a political boundary where there is no natural division whatever, and with the certainty of being in close and undivided neighbourhood with a bitterly hostile state. In short, such an arrangement would render another war at no distant period quite inevitable, and we should in the end be obliged to advance at a great additional expense.

Our western frontier is a more difficult question. If we could occupy Affghanistan as securely as Burmah, it would be well worth our while to do so; but unfortunately there is not in Affghanistan a river navigable to our fleets, and we have learnt by experience that the Affghans are not a race fitted for subjection. Already we are sorely encumbered by the sovereignty over, and vicinity to, a few petty border tribes of Affghan race.

The worst result of our unfortunate Affghan war is the difficulty of now establishing friendly relations in that country. The conduct of the Affghans in the Sikh war was the extremity of folly. They showed enmity—committed, in an irregular way, overt acts of hostility—yet did not materially assist the Sikhs. I do not know whether Dost Mahommed avows the acts of his followers, but the consequence has been the absence of political relations with him. Another circumstance also tends to make our position in regard to the Affghans unpleasant, viz. that we have succeeded the Sikhs in the possession of territory beyond the Indus, recently conquered by the latter, and which the Affghans consider as their patrimony in the possession of an enemy.

To occupy Affghanistan would be out of the question. It is enough that we guard the passes, and that we can at any time, from a basis now near and strong, take military possession of Cabul if the politics of Central Asia become threatening. We must, beyond a doubt, be fully prepared to prevent the occupation of Affghanistan by any other power; and it would be in the highest degree desirable if we could, without loss of dignity, re-establish friendly relations with the Affghans. The Dost might yet be permitted to disavow his sons' and subjects' hostilities in 1849, and to assure us that they are to be construed in a "Pickwickian" sense. The only settlement of our frontier relations upon which any dependence could be placed, and which seems at all feasible, is to get rid of two difficulties at the same time, by bestowing upon the Affghan chief, or some other person or persons of sufficient influence, in some kind of feudal tenure conditional on good behaviour, the most unpleasant and unprofitable of our trans-Indus possessions. The Dost might extract something from the tribes in his own way, and we should be relieved from the civil charge of a tract which we can only manage by a very large military expenditure, by compromises incompatible with our dignity, or by severities inconsistent with our creed. We should still retain possession of the military posts necessary for the security of India. The Affghans would become, in some measure, dependent on us—we should exact from them an obligation to admit no foreign power into Affghanistan—we should pledge ourselves to support them against foreign enemies—the chiefs and the people would look up to us and court our influence—and we might be in some degree arbiters in their more serious quarrels by throwing the weight of our influence in favour of those in the right, and against those in the wrong. The Ameers claim no dignity inconsistent with a feudal inferiority; and if we could establish such a system—fully convince them that having had enough of their territory we no longer desire it—and, in some degree, wipe out the memory of former injuries, Affghanistan might then be in every way that for which nature has designed it—the barrier of India—and closed against all foreign powers.

Whether we deal with Dost Mahommed or with the chiefs of the tribes of the Khyber, there can be no doubt of the principle that the only way of obtaining a hold over mountaineers is to give them a stake in the plains; and that, by gaining such a hold over the possessors of the passes, and keeping your troops in readiness to act on emergencies, you secure the frontier against the entrance of foreign powers at a much less expense than by permanently occupying the mountain country.

Our relations with Persia must be merely diplomatic, and our diplomacy under present circumstances must be solely directed to secure Affghanistan from attack. If diplomacy fails, a naval demonstration would probably suffice to prevent any future attempts on the Affghan territory. What might be our course in the event of Russia attempting to swallow up Persia is a wider question, upon which I shall not at present enter.

We need have no other external relations than those which I have mentioned. Impenetrable mountains and an undisputed ocean render us independent of the best diplomacy.

LONDON :

PRINTED BY WILLIAM CLOWES AND SONS,
STAMFORD STREET.

www.ingramcontent.com/pod-product-compliance
Ingram Content Group UK Ltd.
Pitfield, Milton Keynes, MK11 3LW, UK
UKHW042152280225
455719UK00001B/289